DECA

George Harrison

in the 1970s

Eoghan Lyng

sonicbondpublishing.com

Sonicbond Publishing Limited
www.sonicbondpublishing.co.uk
Email: info@sonicbondpublishing.co.uk

First Published in the United Kingdom 2022
First Published in the United States 2022

British Library Cataloguing in Publication Data:
A Catalogue record for this book is available from the British Library

Copyright Eoghan Lyng 2022

ISBN 978-1-78952-174-0

Typeset in ITC Garamond & ITC Avant Garde
Printed and bound in England

Graphic design and typesetting: Full Moon Media

For flying the banner:

My thanks to Ethan Alexanian, Jason Barnard, Edushkaia Beltranova, Jason Carty, Steven Cockroft, Elena Expósito, Richard Harris, Tom Hunyady, Padraig O'Connor, Marc Ó Foghlú, Sean Macreavy, Ken Michaels and Antony Rotunno.

Which way will you turn
While feeling that our love's not your concern
It's you that decides

Note: For the purpose of this book, *All Things Must Pass* will be pegged as George Harrison's first solo album, with *Wonderwall Music* and *Electronic Sound* being pegged as instrumental offshoot albums recorded during The Beatles tenure.

DECADES | George Harrison in the 1970s

Contents

With Love, From Beatles to Truth

George Harrison was that most curious of characters. Although pencilled as 'the quiet one' of the four Beatles, he was actually the most chameleonic, and certainly the most philosophical of the men who had curated the greatest music of the 1960s. Everything he wrote was shaped by instinct, every quip he delivered was carefully constructed, and everything he played on guitar was delivered with a passion that went beyond professionalism. And yet, cornered in the world's most successful pop sensation, it was growing harder for him to acquiesce to the demands of an audience he simply had no interest in pandering to. Instead, he found solace in India (where he had travelled almost annually since he took his wife Pattie there in 1966). He was also spending more time in the balmy American climes, where Bob Dylan and The Band were enjoying a collaboration based on instinct, intuition and principle. Indeed, *Music From Big Pink* seemed to pinpoint a new form of collaboration, but if Harrison had hoped his better-known group was going to follow Robbie Robertson's lead, he was sure to be disappointed.

By 1968, tensions were simmering within The Beatles. Increasingly perceived as the junior writer of the group, Harrison's desire to record more of his own material was being met with apathy by his bandmates. Aggrieved by the constraints of the band, Harrison made a bold move that radically changed the discourse of the operation, and typified the way he would work as a solo artist. Discouraged by what he perceived as their lack of interest in 'While My Guitar Gently Weeps', Harrison invited Cream superstar Eric Clapton to record the propulsive guitar lick. If the intention was to motivate his bandmates to put their back into the recording, it worked, and Harrison was duly impressed with the piano part McCartney recorded as an intro. Lennon, too was relying on outside counsel, spending more and more time with avant-gardist and girlfriend Yoko Ono, and by the time the band had reconvened for their next album – one they hoped to perform for live audiences – Ono now firmly sat beside the man she was soon to marry. 'It's a question of mutual respect', Clapton surmised. 'I have a great deal of respect for (Harrison) because there have probably been a thousand times when he wanted to quit The Beatles and do something on his own ... Paradoxically, he respects me for having the courage to walk out on groups because I don't like what I am doing. He has often said to me that he does not see me in any band for very long, and I think he has a strange regard for my facing up to impossible situations and just cutting out. But *he* never has'.

Harrison never quit, but there were moments when he questioned his place in the band: 'There used to be a situation where we'd go in (as we did when we were kids), pick up our guitars, all learn the tune and chords, and start talking about arrangements', Harrison recalled. 'But there came a time ... when Paul had fixed an idea in his brain as to how to record one of his songs ... It was taken to the most ridiculous situations, where I'd open my guitar case and go to get my guitar out, and he'd say, 'No, no, we're not doing that yet' ... It got so there was very little to do other than sit around and hear him going, 'Fixing a hole...' with Ringo keeping the time'.

In January 1969, The Beatles congregated at Twickenham Studios to successfully compile a setlist that could be released concurrently as a film and a record. In stark contrast to the band's more ornate approach to studio craft, this was their chance to wipe the slate clean and show themselves as the powerhouse quartet they knew themselves to be – the title *Get Back* had both literal and compositional resonances, and composers John Lennon and Paul McCartney savvily rose to the occasion by adding a roaring, rollicking title track that would double as lead single and conceptual hook. Harrison was writing prolifically, having contributed four numbers to the band's eponymous double album (from here on known as *The White Album*). But faced against two mighty partners, his contributions were steadily being overlooked in favour of undistinguished and disappointing Lennon numbers.

Worse than that, McCartney – now firmly positioned as the band's musical director – had specific visions for his work, which didn't often align with Harrison's. It was at the bassist's insistence that Michael Lindsay-Hogg be granted haven into their headquarters to film and record the band rehearsing, but the bassist may have been less eager had he known the extent to which Harrison's temper would erupt before the cameras. 'I'll play what you want me to play, or I won't play at all if you don't want me to play'. (Peter Jackson's re-edit demonstrated a more nuanced version of the dispute between the two musicians, but it ultimately didn't sting any less than it did on the footage from 1970.) Between these two men – both notably hairier than they'd appeared to the public in 1963 – sat drummer Ringo Starr: clearly upset by the words being thrown by two dear friends. Always the most sensitive band member, Starr was also the most down-to-earth, and it's likely it was he who convinced the other three to perform their new material on the top of Apple Studios.

What the band performed for the public in January 1969 wasn't brilliant, but it compensated by virtue of its ramshackle ferocity; not forgetting the element of surprise. As a finale to the documentary, the performance proved to be an exhilarating close, but it would be the last time these four men appeared in public together. A chance to rebrand the outfit now felt like the last emblems of the group, and wisely the film was released under the more apposite name, *Let It Be*. For contemporary viewers, it felt like a codicil to a decade of incredible work, but the film exemplified the band's lack of organisational skills in kaleidoscopic strokes and palettes. It made the mythology that bit too real for the wide-eyed Beatle fan aching for one final escape into the realm of imagination and wonder.

But before The Beatles had the chance to release this feature, they put their differences aside to record *Abbey Road* – a triumphant album that boasted the band's adept use of harmony vocals ('Because') and synthesizer ('Maxwell's Silver Hammer'), before culminating in a 16-minute medley that sounded like their entire catalogue condensed into a zestful sound collage. Typically, McCartney led the band through the (admittedly jaw-dropping) medley, but that's not to say that Lennon was off his game, as 'I Want You (She's So Heavy)' – a near-eight-minute rocker laced with urgency, understanding and an inspired Santana-esque bridge – proved. And yet, the album's most fondly-remembered number was a Harrison tune. A favourite with stalwarts Shirley Bassey and Frank Sinatra, 'Something' dispelled any unfair notions held against Harrison. With 'Something', Harrison demonstrated an ability that could rival Lennon for canniness and deep-rooted intelligence, yet the song had a viewpoint that was as achingly romantic as the most longing of McCartney's work. Producer George Martin was stunned with the song's maturity and embellished the piece with an exquisite string accompaniment. Most importantly, Harrison's wife Pattie Boyd was touched by the work – something she wore with great pride in the decades to come: 'He told me, in a matter-of-fact way, that he had written it for me. I thought it was beautiful...'.

A precocious guitar player, Harrison had begun enjoying other pursuits, and through his connections to the Krsna movement, he combined his two loves in one form: music. In his eyes, his marriage was verifiable proof of religion: 'All love is part of a universal love. When you love a woman, it's the God in her that you see'.

But for all his idiosyncratic values and practices, he recognised that he belonged in an industry of commerce – a boulder that frequently halted the musician on his journey to inner peace. It was all very well to travel to India in an effort to reconnect with their personal environments (as The Beatles did in 1968 following the death of manager Brian Epstein), but London, legal issues and music always had a way of calling them back to work. And with the band's label Apple rapidly losing money, the four men decided to swallow any pride that was left standing, and hire professional counsel. Paul McCartney's partner Linda Eastman had left America behind for the more bohemian adventures that awaited her in England. Her father Lee was a lawyer, and though his daughter lacked interest in pursuing a career in his field, his soon-to-be son-in-law thought Lee's acumen might come in handy. McCartney suggested Lee Eastman as a possible candidate to his bandmates, although he later conceded that his standing as a relative didn't make him an objective bystander, especially considering the diversity of interests within the group. While McCartney might've been happy to accept another candidate, he pointedly refused to countenance Allen Klein – a man John Lennon figured could help The Beatles out of their predicament. Klein had grit – a trait which won him Harrison's confidence – but McCartney could not be swayed on the matter. In an attempt to level the field, McCartney encouraged Ringo Starr to side with Eastman, but the drummer wouldn't countenance an in-law, no matter how qualified they were, and he too sided with Klein.

What Lennon saw in Klein was a maverick who was willing to achieve what Lennon felt was owed to him and who spoke to him in a language he was able to easily comprehend. Better than that, Klein was a man of action, and for someone of Lennon's own spontaneous disposition, this spoke to him in a way a more orthodox lawyer couldn't. For a time, Lennon and Klein maintained a healthy friendship, and in September 1969, The Beatle informed Klein of his intention to leave the band. Whether it was his interests he was preserving or the band's, isn't relevant for this book, but Klein asked Lennon to put off making an announcement for the time being. There were, he said, too many legal issues to consider, and considering Lennon's impulsive nature, Klein likely thought that he would return to the other three in a matter of weeks. McCartney, Starr and Harrison had all stormed out of sessions over the years, but there was something final about Lennon's decision. He was, after all, the man who assembled the band in Liverpool, and each member of the band enjoyed their closest relationship with him. For McCartney,

Lennon was first his teenage hero and then his musical collaborator; for the drummer, Lennon was a direct peer with whom he could share his most unguarded moments. For Harrison, Lennon was a man who also ached for something more concrete than the immediate gratification a record-breaking album provided. Harrison had worked closely with Lennon in 1966, and together they completed 'Taxman' and 'She Said She Said' for *Revolver*: arguably the most wholly satisfying album in the band's career.

By 1969, the band were bored with songwriting partnerships, and Lennon even suggested that future Beatles songs be credited solely to the man who composed the piece. The barrelling 'Cold Turkey' – released in October 1969 – was credited to Lennon alone, and featured Starr alone of the other Beatles. Instead, Hamburg favourite Klaus Voorman played bass, while Eric Clapton played the pummelling guitar lick that echoed the mania that comes with heroin withdrawal. Lennon could never have issued such a raw track with the band, but by this point, the 30-year-old rhythm player was beyond caring. It wasn't that he was tired of working with The Beatles – he simply didn't need to work with them to produce music that excited him. Klein and McCartney may have wished otherwise, but for Lennon, there was no turning back.Brokenhearted, McCartney had no choice but to respect the decision, and all agreed to keep it quiet for the time being.

They still had one last album to release, although the record – and more pressingly the film – were uncomfortable for Harrison to acknowledge. In his mind, they symbolised everything that contributed to the demise of the band: opinions he held until the end of his life. But he could take comfort from the fact that he got to jam with American keyboardist Billy Preston during the sessions, which added another element to the band's sound. Guesting on 'Get Back' and 'Don't Let Me Down', Preston decorated the ramshackle recordings with a professional polish that helped settle an otherwise anarchic-sounding single. Friends in real life, Harrison and Preston continued to work together throughout the 1970s, and the guitarist could happily depend on the keyboardist's soaring harmony lines when the pair collaborated on the ill-fated Dark Horse tour in 1974.

Yet just as Harrison was climbing up in the world of rock stardom, he decided to take a step away from that orbit and produce an album of Vedic chants. If the 'Hare Krishna Mantra' single had an agenda, it wasn't a commercial one, but Harrison felt strongly enough about the music to record it himself at Apple Studios. The song was hardly verbose (It consists of a 16-word Sanskrit Maha Mantra, repeated during the verse and chorus), but the emotion was infectious and offered the London-based ISKCON devotees exposure they would never have received from another member of The Beatles. Characteristically generous, Harrison appeared in the background, clearly moved (and possibly humbled) by the unbridled devotion being sung into the microphone. Releasing the track that August, Harrison committed himself completely to the movement, understanding the commitment and joy that was needed to reach that point of fulfilment: 'It wasn't until the experience of the sixties really hit', Harrison recalled in 1982. 'You know, having been successful and meeting everybody we thought worth meeting, and finding out they weren't worth meeting, and having had more hit records than everybody else and having done it bigger than everybody else – it was like reaching the top of a wall and then looking over and seeing that there's so much more on the other side. So I felt it was part of my duty to say, 'Oh, okay, maybe you are thinking this is all you need – to be rich and famous – but actually it isn't".

Fuelling him in a way The Beatles never truly had, Harrison worked on an album with the congregation: later released as *The Radha Krsna Temple* in 1971. His production was sparse, admirable and filled with tremendous reverence, but the album only had a limited appeal. Much better was his single-turned-anthem 'My Sweet Lord', which exposed the immediacy of the movement in a world of longing and false answers. But Harrison was entitled to grin at Radha Krsna Temple on *Top of The Pops* – his newfound friends were enjoying the spotlight with some of the trendiest, most facile artists in the industry. Better still, the mantra was played over the PA at the Isle of White, just as Harrison's peer and confidante Bob Dylan was about to take to the stage. Already Harrison's influence was taking a hold on the world, but like many of his great triumphs (including his tenure as a movie producer), it was done in the shadows and far away from the spotlight.

Comedy was swiftly emerging as a new voice of rebellion. Michael Palin – regularly pencilled as the most accomplished of the six Python actors – was pleased to hear that Paul McCartney would interrupt Abbey Road recording sessions to catch the latest episode of *Monty Python's Flying Circus*. Palin elaborated in 2003: 'The other story – which I have no reason to disprove – was that George Harrison says he sent a congratulatory note to the BBC. So right from the very start, there was this connection with the best band in the world and our little band of comedy thesps'.

Around this time (December 1969), Delaney and Bonnie Bramlett were performing in Britain. Captivated by their material, Harrison joined them onstage in Bristol, and performed with the duo for five of the tour's six nights. Like Lennon, Harrison held very few positive memories of his secondary school days, and was more likely to play the part of the rebel than the more-disciplined learner. But as an adult, he proved to be an adept – even admirable – student, and devoted hours (even days) to improving areas of his life he felt needed sprucing. Indeed, Harrison spent hours fine-tuning his songs, days working out arrangements, and years dedicated to the sitar. Slide guitar was his newest challenge, and under the influence of Delaney & Bonnie, he happened upon a new form of musical expression. He was free to play as he liked, and with Eric Clapton to bounce off, there was a liveliness to Harrison's playing, unheard during the Twickenham sessions eleven months earlier. He was undergoing changes – some of them brilliant, many of them painful. His relationship with McCartney had soured, and it would be years before the two men could enjoy each other's company again.

Harrison was also facing a trauma much closer to home. His mother, Louise Harrison (née French) was suffering from cancer, and much of Harrison's emotional energy was understandably taken up with her. No band, however tremendous, can compare to the death of a loved one, and in the context of Louise' illness, the breakup of the band must have seemed trivial to Harrison. Music, merriment and laughter would serve him well whenever a breakup or bereavement awaited him in the years ahead.

...And Then There Was 1970...

The Beatles could be forgiven for starting their career on a parody number, particularly when you consider how jolly 'Cry For A Shadow' still sounds. Written as a pastiche of Hank Marvin's guitar-playing, the pounding instrumental was put to tape on 22 June 1961 and holds the distinction of being one of the earliest songs George Harrison offered the band. By January 1970, Harrison had grown into a more assured writer, and was finally primed to attack the ego that was steadily growing within the band's orbit. There was no chance that Lennon was interested in contributing to 'I Me Mine', but Harrison could still rely on contributions from McCartney and Starr to complete the song. Long-considered the band's in-house keyboardist, McCartney added a haunting organ line to 'I Me Mine' – a scorching rocker later sullied by an unwanted string accompaniment that drove the listener's focus away from the lyrics. Better again, old school friends Harrison and McCartney threw themselves into the chorus, fashioning a bridge that was every bit as exhilarating – and infinitely more sincere – than the pastiche number they recorded in Germany all those years ago. Bookending The Beatles' career with two of his very own numbers, Harrison now packed up his guitar, and left the band behind him.

Having just bought the Victorian mansion Friar Park in Henley-on-Thames, Harrison was spending much of his free time there. The garden was expansive, the rooms were many, and he enjoyed having people over to visit. As the decade wore on, the house would prove to be equal-parts studio, confessional, shelter and amenity for the guitarist, and he risked losing it in 1979, having put it up as collateral to finance Monty Python's feature film *Life of Brian*. Harrison – much like Lennon – had found The Beatles most recent recording sessions troubling.

Vacating the *Get Back/Let It Be* sessions, the guitarist turned to the very instrument that had once channelled his more primordial feelings, for the storming 'Wah Wah'. Compiling nearly ten years of anger into a five-minute rocker, 'Wah Wah' explored a darker side of the guitarist, and naturally, he didn't record it with The Beatles. Instead, it was saved for his debut album as a singer-songwriter (He had issued two instrumental albums in the late-1960s), where it sat incongruously beside a convoy of elegies and canticles. Nonetheless, 'Wah Wah' was a belting track, and sounded excellent live, particularly at *The Concert For Bangladesh* in 1971.

Straight from the off, Harrison ached to distance himself from the Beatles' legacy and create a new one entirely. Yet the harder he pushed for the result, the greater the distance he felt between himself and the crowds that paid to hear him perform 'Something' as he had in 1969. Although long-considered his finest work inside The Beatles, the original recording came with a McCartney bass line many considered to be needlessly propulsive: 'I think George thought my bass-playing was a little bit busy', McCartney recalled in 2000. 'Again, from my side, I was trying to contribute the best I could, but maybe it was his turn to tell me I was too busy'. Harrison said much the same in 1974: 'Paul is a fine bass player, but he's a bit overpowering at times'. He continued in this particular vein to admit that he'd rather work with Lennon over McCartney before condemning the imprint The Beatles had left on him: 'Why do they want to see if there is a Beatle George? I don't say I'm Beatle George ... Gandhi says create and preserve the image of your choice. The image of my choice is not Beatle George'.

However they felt about the Beatles bassist, Harrison and Lennon still enjoyed a cordial friendship, and Harrison wound up performing on Lennon's 'Instant Karma' in January 1970. Caught up in the excitement of the track, Lennon delivered the most authentic vocal of his career and the single ranks amongst the best songs he ever wrote. Moreover, the single featured legendary music alumnus Phil Spector as its producer: who reportedly joined Lennon when The Beatle informed him that he'd 'written a monster'.

Lennon and Spector enjoyed a camaraderie that was genuine, which led Lennon to ask him to sift through the *Get Back* tapes that had been lying dormant for the best part of a year. Seemingly uninterested in honouring The Beatles desire to strip themselves bare on record, Spector added orchestral flourishes to the work, which horrified McCartney, especially considering the yearning he'd aimed for on 'The Long And Winding Road'.

Typically, Lennon had a different view to his former songwriting partner: '(Spector) was given the shittiest load of badly recorded shit with a lousy feeling toward it, ever. And he made something out of it. He did a great job'. Posterity has painted McCartney as the one who was least keen to give up on The Beatles, but even *he* recognised that the band he'd led in the 1960s had no place in the 1970s. Moreover, the time spent with a wife and two children had opened the bassist up to a new perspective: a narrative he proudly opened to the world on his eponymous lo-fi debut. There, free from the constraints of Beatledom, McCartney elected to demonstrate the little pleasures he found in everyday household objects ('Junk'), before celebrating the glories of love on the superlative and soul-bearing 'Maybe I'm Amazed'. Compared to The Beatles' more-lush work, the album was much more sparse, and critics were quick to attack its more-rustic production design – but by then, McCartney was beyond caring. In the Q+A that accompanied the album, the songwriter proceeded to place the importance of his family over any future work with his bandmates. Fed up with carrying the silence, McCartney called an end to the band on 17 April 1970.

The man who'd written The Beatles' first single was now waving goodbye to the legacy, and though this action was one Lennon took umbrage with, the action nonetheless held a certain poetry – for now, McCartney had a vocation, and family was as much an identity to him as peacekeeping was to Lennon and spirituality was to Harrison. And in each of their ways, these three men incorporated their chosen identities into their craft with due importance and attention, regardless of the zeitgeist of the time. If McCartney had any concerns about recording a nursery rhyme, he never showed them promoting Wings' 'Mary Had A Little Lamb', and whatever misgivings Lennon had towards violence, he nonetheless applauded the Irish Republican Movement on his otherwise disappointing album *Some Time In New York City*.

So that left Ringo Starr alone to furnish a whole new image for himself and one that predictably didn't take off. And yet he enjoyed some significant success as a singles artist in the early-1970s, capturing a market based on instinct, not art. Such was his value as a friend, the Beatle songwriters gladly put aside any misgivings they had for one another, to each contribute a song to the drummer's 1973 meisterwerk.

Then there was Harrison – always that bit quieter and purportedly less-accepting than the others. Caught in the intensity of his surroundings, later Beatles albums had shown a songwriter demonstrating a fondness for the change of weather ('Here Comes The Sun') and the servitude to a god who had brought that change to the world ('Long, Long, Long'). Here, in Friar Park, Harrison had the garden to appreciate both virtues, and the hours he spent walking through greenery, were ones he preferred to those containing the board meetings that had changed four Liverpool musicians into business moguls.

Through papers and lawyers, The Beatles were growing more singular in their visions and more forceful in their individual voices. But Harrison had long harnessed a voice, which was one he could present wholesale on a triple album commonly regarded as the most dazzling of any solo effort. And much like the skills he'd learnt as a gardener, it was an album borne from pruning, shaping and perfecting.

But he was no less affected by the breakup of a band that had taken up much of his creative and intellectual energy. His friendship with McCartney – the man who'd introduced him to Lennon back in those halcyon days of Liverpool buses – was disintegrating through a convoy of court cases, couriers and charades. And though he granted Lennon support on his solo albums, Harrison was soon to find that his gestures weren't always reciprocated. Faith, as ever, guided him through this water of uncertainty, and much like the prayers, he chanted with gusto, Harrison's greatest strength came from the very same exercise: singing.

It's easy to romanticise the end of The Beatles as some Shakespearean tragedy, but the breakup was ultimately one of growth and not of spite. Together they had enjoyed tremendous fortune, and whatever fortunes these men would earn could not have arisen, but for the decade they'd spent so productively in Abbey Road. Longtime confidante and session bassist Klaus Voorman offered a philosophical perspective in 2020: 'Those ten years were more than enough. Ringo would have stayed with the band; he loved everybody. But the rest, there was lots of anger, fights – they couldn't have done it any longer because they were all in completely different directions. *Abbey Road*, it's a beautiful LP, but ... from a feeling point of view, it wasn't right to do it. They had to do it because they had obligations to the record company. But they did it really professional and fantastic, and that's what makes a good band, you know?'.

All Things Must Pass

Personnel:
George Harrison: vocals, guitar, slide guitar, harmonica
Eric Clapton, Peter Frampton, Dave Mason: guitar
Pete Drake: pedal steel guitar
Pete Ham, Tom Evans, Joey Molland: acoustic rhythm guitar
Billy Preston: piano, keyboards, organ
Gary Wright: piano, electric piano, keyboards, organ
Gary Brooker, Tony Ashton: piano
Bobby Whitlock: backing vocals, piano, organ
Klaus Voormann, Carl Radle: bass
Jim Price: trumpet

Bobby Keys: saxophone
Ringo Starr: drums, tambourine
Alan White, Jim Gordon: drums
Mike Gibbins: tambourine
Record Label: Apple
Recorded: May-October 1970 at EMI, Trident and Apple Studios, London.
Produced by George Harrison and Phil Spector
Release Dates: UK: 30 November 1970, US: 27 November 1970
Chart placings: UK: 1, US: 1
Running Time: 106:00

But the breakup left a mark on the group. 'Everybody had gone through that', Harrison sighed in *The Beatles Anthology*. 'Ringo had left at one point. I know John wanted out. It was a very, very difficult, stressful time, and being filmed having a row as well was terrible. I got up and I thought, 'I'm not doing this anymore. I'm out of here'. So I got my guitar and went home, and that afternoon wrote 'Wah-Wah'.

Together, Harrison and Billy Preston collaborated on Doris Troy's eponymous album: an Apple record duly released in September 1970. Discussing her work with author Simon Leng, Troy could see the influence gospel had on Harrison: 'I think he had been involved in soul music for years – he listened to it, he loved it, and that's what made him want to do it. I wasn't actually introducing him to the stuff; he already knew it. The Beatles as a whole listened to black music; a lot of their soul and feelings came from American music'. Harrison's greatest tribute to soul would arrive five years later. But for now, he had a triple album to record.

From the moment Harrison started to hone his craft with The Beatles, the seeds of his Homeric debut were being sown. Early compositions like 'Isn't It A Pity' and 'All Things Must Pass' are extremely confident in their ambition, signalling the innate fears that exist in each of us. On 'If Not For You', the slide arpeggio has an almost ceremonial sense of presence, while 'Hear Me Lord' shifts from rustic blues to swirling symphonies, climaxing with augmented – even operatic – pose. This was music written for occasion; chords that demanded to be dissected, from a guitar player who didn't wish to be seen. He was embracing change, hiding from the public, and exploring the choices that had drawn him to this moment of calm. His son Dhani Harrison told *Esquire*: 'I'm really trying to draw everyone into the feeling of what it must have been like for him to start off at 27, renovating a house that took him the rest of his life, and at the same time, his band had broken up, he had Hare Krishnas living here, he was separating from his wife, his mother passed away during the making of the record – it was a lot of really spiritual moments for my dad with this record'.

Working as a solo artist thereafter, Harrison had to bow to no one's agenda but his own, but his decision to start his career with a triple album was a particularly brave one. Not that there was a shortage of material, and Spector remembered with glee the quality of the catalogue that was being presented to him: 'I went to George's Friar Park estate, and he said, 'I have a few ditties for you to hear'. It was endless! He had literally hundreds of songs, and each one was better than the other'.

Harrison was even more direct in 1992: 'I didn't have many tunes on Beatles records. Doing an album like *All Things Must Pass* was like going to the bathroom and letting it out'. That Harrison could produce 23 songs was remarkable enough, but what elevated this folk album into the high echelons of 1970s rock, was that he recognised the vitality of Spector's production style, simultaneously lacing the spiritual focus with typically-dry Northern humour. Between the more celebrated and lofty-sounding anthems came a selection of lighter, more jocular work, and the breadth of material – from the highbrow to the bawdy – helped to make *All Things Must Pass* a commercial triumph. Born out of the demise of the Liverpool band, the album typified candour, perspective and personal growth. And through the heartbreak came laughter, as Harrison adorned his album cover with four garden gnomes: each a representation of a Beatle. Outside his garden, the bearded creatures held a more mythological status, but deep in the heart of his newly-furnished abode, Harrison captured the group at their most flippant, fragile and childlike.

McCartney might have been the most reluctant to abandon The Beatles, but he'd completed an excellent debut and was set to follow it up with an even better album. Harrison seemed easier with the idea of the band breaking up (He remembered the band as 'like a straitjacket'), but there's no doubt that he missed the camaraderie and lamented the lost friendships the breakup had cost him. As a parting gift to the band – not forgetting the fans all over the world for whom The Beatles had represented something much greater – he decided to commemorate them in a way that only he could: 'Originally, when we took the photo, I had these old Bavarian gnomes which I thought I would put there, like kinda... John, Paul, George and Ringo. Gnomes are very popular in

Europe and these gnomes were made in about 1860'. Seated between the four gnomes was Harrison, now very much the gardener he would continue to be for the rest of his life. It was less the image of an artist purveying the works of a lesser artist but more the contented smile of an older man happy to leave the institution of rock behind him. Comforted by the greenery that surrounded him, Harrison could journey forward in life, safe in the knowledge that the garden was there to shelter him when he needed it to.

Contrary to popular opinion, *All Things Must Pass* was not rock's first triple album but followed the equally triumphant Woodstock soundtrack onto the charts. In his own way, Harrison was carrying on the narrative the soundtrack spun but laced the work with a largeness that could only be done in the studio. Everywhere we turn, the 1970 original envelopes into a cascade of guitar licks, pushing the boundaries of volume on an album that was almost entirely based on journey. His lyrics were taking a turn from the more commercially-oriented songs The Beatles were writing, but his commitment to studio craft was as unwavering as ever.

The album does feature one other Beatle – Ringo Starr – although the extent to which the drummer contributed to the album differs depending on who is telling the story. When I interviewed Alan White for *CultureSonar*, the powerhouse Yes percussionist noted that Harrison and Starr played together on one track: 'The only track I saw him on was playing tambourine on 'My Sweet Lord'.

For anyone studying the quality of sound that emanated from the speakers, perhaps the most admirable aspect of the final mix was the diversity of musicianship. In the 1960s, albums were either the product of bands or stellar studio players, and though there were some moments of overlap, it was done as an invitation from one property to the other. *All Things Must Pass* was a different animal, collating the textures of both schools to create an entirely new form of work.

If it wasn't the most accessible solo Beatle record (John Lennon's work thrived on immediacy, and Paul McCartney demonstrated a passion for melody, between the more idiosyncratic vignettes on his first album), it *was* the most well-thought-out and certainly the most lyrical. No matter how many keyboardists, drummers or guitarists play in unison, the album's central focus are the words themselves – every syllable delivered with passion for a crusade that was now becoming more important to Harrison than had been the band that led to it. Nostalgia could be its own reward, but Harrison took strength from the prospect of starting everything over.

Stemming from a writing session with Bob Dylan, 'I'd Have You Anytime' was a bold choice to open the album. In the timeline of the album's history, most artists would've chosen a louder track to grab the listener's attention. Instead, the slow, sparsely-written piece offered listeners momentary respite before the indelible 'My Sweet Lord' kicked the album into more commercial territories. But the song – complete with a Dylan/Harrison credit – also made the breadth of Harrison's influence clear to dissenters – McCartney may have underestimated Harrison's abilities, but the writer of 'The Times They Are A-Changin'', didn't. Ultimately, the song works brilliantly in establishing Harrison's confidence, and the singer seems to be enjoying the chance to breathe before bludgeoning into some of the record's harder, more-detailed vocals.

It has often been remarked that 'I'd Have You Anytime' was put on the album because of who co-wrote the words, but the slower, more-methodological pace made it an inspired choice for album opener. The Beatles had traditionally opened their albums with a turbocharged rocker ('It Won't Be Long', 'Help!' and Harrison's 'Taxman'), but the unhurried 'I'd Have You Anytime' offers a taste as to the direction the album would follow. The vocals are solemn, the chorus is steady, and the electric guitars follow a fastidious direction that weaves with the verses. Instead of performing a fiery guitar lick that had long been his preference with Cream, Eric Clapton played with greater poise, recognising the power of the words sung in front of him. But it didn't hurt that the song bore a Dylan co-write, which must have given Harrison a needed boost as he released his first fully-realised solo effort.

Then it's onto 'My Sweet Lord' – the song that best typified Harrison's spiritual mission statement and proved to be the most popular number of his solo career. Like 'I'd Have You Anytime' before it, 'My Sweet Lord' is an acoustic number, but the piece rocks more following the entrance of a punchy slide lick. What follows is brilliant – imitating the vocal harmonies, the slide presents its melody directly and immediately, instilling familiarity in the ears of those who heard it. By the time the vocals kicked in, listeners were struck by the work; by the time it came to the close, they were singing along to it. As the song wears on, the elation grows – by the closing chorus, Harrison has cloaked these feelings in something greater still, and the answers (such as they are) remain as elusive at the close as they were at the beginning. But it's clear from the songs that it's not the answers that fuel the excitement, but the questions that have fuelled the singer:

I really wanna know you
Really wanna go with you
Really wanna show you Lord
That it won't take long, my Lord
(Hallelujah)

His demeanour is joyous, and the joy that carries him to the climax is the same joy that started him on his course. Better still, he didn't discriminate between religions, but rather ached to call attention to the excitement of religion – fittingly, the song has almost as many 'Hare rama's as it does 'hallelujah's. With an uplifting chorus, 'My Sweet Lord' was also produced with great attention to the air existing between the chiming chords. The slide is breezily performed, and the passion that emanates from the vocal only grows more noticeable with every passing verse.

Harrison's breakthrough hit began life as an exercise in meditation as the guitarist busied himself backstage at a Delaney & Bonnie concert in Copenhagen. But what finally emerged was his truest and most commercial homage to God. As it happened, the Edwin Hawkins Singers were enjoying a gospel hit with 'Oh Happy Day': a zesty reworking of an 18th-century hymn: 'It really just knocked me out, the idea of that song, and I just felt a great feeling of the Lord', Harrison said in Keith Badman's book *The Beatles: Off the Record 2 – The Dream Is Over*. 'So, I thought, 'I'll write another 'Oh Happy Day'', which became 'My Sweet Lord''.

Purportedly written with Billy Preston in mind, Harrison produced a version of the song for the keyboardist's excellent *Encouraging Words* (1970). Preston had played a part in the song's creative process, and acquits himself quite well to it (Appropriately, Preston sang it at the *Concert for George* in 2002).

But it was always destined to end up on Harrison's debut album, though it was harder to convince him to issue it as a single. It was at Spector's urging that the song was finally released as a double A-side with 'Isn't It A Pity'. Encased between the chiming acoustics and a tremendous slide hook, came a chorus of vocals (each sung by Harrison, and credited to the George O Hara singers) – each vocal determined to carry the hidden chant to its final destination.

Harrison was deservedly proud of the track, but he was wary of the spiritual apotheosis; not forgetting the death threats The Beatles had received in 1966 when Lennon compared their tremendous popularity to that of Jesus. Ultimately, Harrison felt uneasy unleashing the piece out into the world: 'I was sticking my neck out on the chopping block because now I would have to live up to something', he wrote in *I Me Mine*. 'But at the same time, I thought, 'Nobody's saying it; I wish somebody else was doing it''.

The standard of material was never in doubt, but it was the album's shimmering production style that ensured its success with a transatlantic public. Between the chiming guitars, angelic backing vocals and aphorisms came a monolithic soundscape that served as much as an identity as it did another instrument. Together, Harrison and Spector made a great team, and in their combined efforts, they crafted a work that was tight, punchy, yet unrelenting in its resolve. It was Spector who encouraged Harrison to pursue the huge, spacious sound that laced the work, culminating in a triple record that sounded incredible in execution and piercing in ambition.

For all the technical guitar patterns that burst with colour, contradiction and compassion, the album still sounds incredibly humble, and the anthems 'Ballad Of Sir Frankie Crisp (Let It Roll)' and 'Hear Me Lord' show a lyricist with an impressive lack of vanity. Whatever the ferocity of the musicianship, the singer never shows himself as anything more than grateful for the pleasures, pastures and opportunities his God has given him. Best of all, the album boasted the fiery, vaguely Hawaiian guitar sound that reared its head all over Harrison's work. 'One time he asked me if I would teach him how to play slide', Delaney Bramlett recalled, 'and later, George said I'd taught him how to play it. Well, he did make that statement, but I didn't teach him anything. George already knew how to play guitar, he just wanted to know my technique, what I thought about it and what I did. All I did was teach him my style of playing'.

In many ways, 'My Sweet Lord' typifies the pace of the album, but it does include another gorgeous opus that could just as easily have been published as a poem, such was the strength of the lyric. In a country where riffs were king, Harrison's pastoral 'All Things Must Pass' – slower-moving and soaked in Robbie Robertson's influence – was a decidedly different type of beast, exploring the changes that bind nature and humans together:

Sunset doesn't last all evening
A mind can blow those clouds away
After all this, my love is up and must be leaving
It's not always gonna be this grey

In its primitive form, it was a stunning exhibition of Harrison's potential. But under Spector's eye, the urgency changed like an alarm bell – thunderous horns and fulminative drums latching onto the work as if inhabiting the sudden changes of weather. Indeed, the entire song was a tightrope over a narrow valley, but it was an endearing walk: the luminous beauty surrounding the jagged edges of an uncertain terrain. Exceptionally well-produced, the track ends with a stunning collage of massed trumpets, directing the vocalist back to his safe haven.

Much as there was love and laughter, there was also a darkness to the work, and it doesn't take a degree in Beatle studies to recognise that 'Run Of The Mill' was Harrison's way of ejecting himself from the group. There is, however, more to 'Run Of The Mill' than throwing digs at McCartney – the lyric confronts the changes that were surrounding Harrison, and challenges him to accept the directions the world was presenting him. Nothing about his appearance or demeanour reminded anyone of the charming – if caustic – kid playing guitar in *A Hard Day's Night*. 'Run Of The Mill' was his way of tipping the scales, and by throwing out the lies (or mistruths) that had followed him for years, he was offering his fans one chance to gauge the narrative from his perspective. There are few Spector-like hallmarks – the guitars are clean and fresh-sounding, the vocals are sung clearly, as if presented to a hall of listeners searching for a reminder to quieten themselves, and the bucolic and beautiful brass section are presented with great restraint. Better still were the words, displaying an appreciation for the power and malleability the English language is so capable of. Likening the lyric to a poem, the ballad has proven to be a favourite among many listeners: Harrison's second wife Olivia among them. 'He just lived by his deeds', Spector recalled in 2011. 'He was spiritual, and you knew it, and there was no salesmanship involved. It made you spiritual being around him'.

Rock is the operative word for the album, not least on the towering 'Art Of Dying': a propulsive guitar-heavy piece featuring some of Harrison's most animal-like arpeggios. Driven by barrelling drums and a furious garage-like riff, 'Art Of Dying' was an unusually raucous affair for Harrison, bolstered by the brass ricocheting around the microphones. Chiming perfectly with the rise of British metal, Harrison had been toying with the number since 1966, although he had delayed recording and releasing the song, fearing it was that bit too far out for public consumption. Dusting it up for the album, he laid down the rocker with at least eight men by his side, thereby creating a wall of turbocharged energy and force. Drummer

Phil Collins reportedly stood in for a session, but his contributions were discarded, much to the teenager's disappointment. Nevertheless, his connection to the album only helped to secure his place with Genesis: a burgeoning prog rock band for whom Collins would serve as both drummer and singer.

Harrison had already released one instrumental album in 1968 (*Wonderwall Music*) and another in 1969 (*Electronic Sound*), but the idea of putting an instrumental section on *All Things Must Pass* has been perceived by many critics as needless indulgence in the years since its release. It's difficult to imagine another mainstream artist willing to devote two sides of vinyl to a series of angular guitar licks, but Harrison deemed the *Apple Jam* disc worthy of release, so he tacked it onto *All Things Must Pass*. A guitar player above all other trades in life, Harrison had more than merited the chance to unveil a collection of jams, and the recordings are as wild as the songs are carefully calibrated. This was his chance to let loose and jam with Clapton: his closest friend and sparring buddy.

No, they didn't sound organised *per sé*, but the considerable joys of the *Apple Jam* section lie not in its cohesion but in the raw, untethered guitar interactions that occur between Harrison and Clapton. 'Out Of The Blue' opens the record with an interplay that seems reverent, even respectful of the other's talents. But by the time we get to 'Thanks For The Pepperoni', any sense of sportsmanlike gestures have been discarded for a collision of reverb – every man eager to reach that finish line, no matter the noise they make in the process. But between these rockers comes 'It's Johnny's Birthday': a pleasant, pub-like rendition of Bill Martin and Phil Coulter's 'Congratulations'. Harrison changed the lyrics to suit his friend, who was now celebrating his 30th birthday, and in some ways, this comical vignette best surmised his feelings towards the jam. As Harrison explained in 2000, 'For the jams, I didn't want to just throw (them) in the cupboard, and yet at the same time it wasn't part of the record – that's why I put it on a separate label to go in the package as a kind of bonus'.

If the fans didn't want to listen to the jams, then they didn't have to, but it was nice for Harrison to relax after baring his soul over four sides of vinyl. Lennon too was gearing himself to write a cleansing record that exorcised the failings of his education and the excitement of his new marriage, while McCartney (famously more reserved in interview than his bandmates) was also exposing a more vulnerable side to himself, as evinced on the magnificent 'Maybe I'm Amazed'. It seemed that the

1970s demanded a greater level of authenticity from rock than had been expected of their 1960s predecessors, but soon the three men would have to face groups like Pink Floyd, Yes and Emerson, Lake & Palmer: progressive composers who would push the barriers of narrative rock to greater heights in the years ahead. Therein lay the dichotomy – while the rock press demanded truth from their artists, listeners gravitated to a form of songcraft that was richer in sonics and flourishes.

As it happened, McCartney was the solo Beatle who best bridged the gap between the two divisions, and rock centrepieces *Ram, Band On The Run* and *Venus and Mars* enjoyed a footing with both camps of listeners. Unsurprisingly, McCartney enjoyed a solo career that far eclipsed his colleague's efforts, but though Lennon may have been bothered by this development, Harrison seemed unfazed by it. Throughout the decade, Harrison showed scant interest in Wings, feeling that they were 'inoffensive' and directed at the adolescent audience he had long wished to escape from. His relationship with McCartney preceded his friendships with Lennon and Starr, and like many relationships that jump from childhood into adulthood, Harrison endured many moments of friction with the bassist. But they always stood by each other in times of hardship, and neither man was afraid to say he loved the other whenever a journalist asked how he felt about the other.

From Bobby Whitlock's wistful piano playing to Pete Drake's vibrant pedal steel, the album allowed each of the session players the freedom to perform with tremendous flair and flavour, each of them rewarded in the final mix. The production is gorgeous, culminating in a tapestry that grows even more powerful with every added instrument. Not everyone who performed on the album was familiar with Harrison's metiér: Drake being one of them. 'His name, you know, just didn't ring any bells – well, I'm just a hillbilly, you know', Drake recalled. 'Anyway, I ended up going to London for a week where we did the album *All Things Must Pass*'.

Drake may not have been familiar with Harrison's work, but guitarist Joey Molland – himself a man from Liverpool – was glad of the chance to play with his hero: '(Badfinger) played on most of it', Molland revealed to *Penny Black*'s Lisa Torem. 'We'd just go in and it would be a bit of a blur because we'd just go in at 11 in the morning and start working on songs, and after we played on 'My Sweet Lord', 'Beware Of Darkness', 'Isn't It A Pity' and 'Wah-Wah'; just loads of song after song after song. 'What Is Life'; all of it, really. Even on the jams, we'd just beat along on the acoustics. It was great, great fun'.

Guitarist Peter Frampton recalled: 'George says, 'Phil wants more acoustics. Can you bring your guitar, and we'll have an afternoon of just you and me? We'll overdub on whatever he needs'. That's when we went to Abbey Road, where all The Beatles stuff was done, and sat on two stools, me and George, looking in the control room at Phil Spector'.

Harrison was looking everywhere for inspiration and found it in his garden. History was an arm's reach away; greenery even nearer, and he was constantly struck by the poetry that surrounded him. Aching to bring it all together, he summoned the strength to commit it all to tape:

Let it roll across the floor
Through the hall and out the door
To the fountain of perpetual mirth
Let it roll for all it's worth

That mantra cements 'Ballad Of Sir Frankie Crisp (Let It Roll)' – an enjoyable if lightweight tune that would've serviced an everyday pop artist looking for a hit (It revels in whimsy, which might explain why it fit so well onto the soundtrack of *How I Met Your Mother*: a mainstream 2000s sitcom that boasted an interestingly diverse soundtrack). More substantial was his rendition of 'If Not For You', which marked a tradition of covers Harrison would put on his albums. More often than not, they were among the most accomplished, but that simply showed how much faith Harrison had in the songs others had written for him. And with words of Dylan's calibre, Harrison could relax and sing to his heart's content.

Harrison's 'Awaiting On You All' is a lacerating treatise on catholic relations in the search for spiritual absolution. In his eyes, the papacy stood for capitalism, denigrating from the worth of the Lord he loved. Rather than confining God to a 'passport' or a 'visa', Harrison considers the Lord's voice to be an all-encompassing one, pivoting from the centre of the universe to the hearts of the millions aching for a sign. As always, Harrison's work carried a message, and the album demonstrates a fondness for human interaction before warning them of the dangers they are thrusting on themselves.

Throughout the album, there is delirium, devastation and disgust: much of it aimed at himself as much as at other people. 'Isn't It A Pity' carried the most damning verdict, and the track – sprawling, sincere and singular – foreshadows a world where the impossibility of peace is lessened by the lenience of man's more-altruistic tendencies. Cheeky as ever, Harrison's ballad ends with a soaring chorus of gospel singers, each of them chewing their 'nah nah nah' with spirited relish. Some commentators later felt that it resembled the closing coda of McCartney's 'Hey Jude', but if there was wagging on Harrison's part, at least it was done with jocularity and general goodwill. (The song remains one of Harrison's most extraordinary lyrical achievements, but his decision to reprise the piece later on the record was a curious one, not least because it drew listeners back to the repeated motifs on *Sgt. Pepper's Lonely Hearts Club Band* and *The White Album*. But then again, maybe that was the point.)

For all the pithy, cerebral songs that make up the *All Things Must Pass* track list, the album also features a number of visceral, comedic numbers. 'I Dig Love' demonstrates the songwriter's more docile side, segueing from a blues terrain to a bouncier bridge, complete with nonsensical verse and rhyme. Then there was 'Apple Scruffs': Harrison's valedictorian anthem for the enthusiastic Beatle fans who frequented Apple Corps.

More appropriately, pizza opus 'Thanks For The Pepperoni' proved to be a fittingly tasty treat and had a title lifted directly from the mouth of American stand-up comedian Lenny Bruce. Little over a year after the 'miserable' *Get Back* sessions, Harrison, the solo artist, was determined to have as good a time as he could muster. Yes, it was all work, but there was also much play. 'If Eddie (Klein) did anything wrong, there'd be half an hour of jokes and laughing at his expense', bassist Klaus Voorman remembered. `Cruel for Eddie, perhaps, but great fun for everybody else'.

Ensconced at Abbey Road, Harrison was surrounded by a wide circle of friends, colleagues and fellow musicians. Having encouraged The Beatles to utilise Eric Clapton and Billy Preston during some of the later sessions, Harrison was hungry to work with a grander circuit of musicians. Abbey Road tape operator John Leckie – who would later produce Beatle disciples XTC and The Stone Roses – felt that the change of pace suited Harrison: 'Phil Spector was fantastic', Leckie told *We Are Cult*. 'Very funny man, one of the first gigs I had. I think Phil brought a lot out of George Harrison, saying, let's have all our mates in, 24 people playing on it rather than just four Beatles. Eric Clapton brought the Derek and The Dominos guys along, so there was a lot of great guitars and equipment, very peace and love'.

Spector encouraged Harrison to push himself as a vocalist and wrote to the songwriter to explain his rationale: 'I really feel that your voice has got to be heard throughout the album so that the greatness of the songs can really come through. We can't cover you up too much (and there really is no need to), although, as I said, I'm sure excellent mixes can be obtained with just the proper amount of time spent on each one'.

Orchestral director John Barham enjoyed working with the solo Beatle: 'I stayed at Friar Park while we did the preparatory work for the orchestrations of 'All Things Must Pass'. We discussed arrangement details, as George wanted them to be finalised before the session. George didn't want any surprises at the last moment in the studio – he didn't like last-minute changes and preferred things to be well thought out in advance'; the greatest, most emotive guitar-playing came from Harrison himself – not the rollicking guitar line that opened 'What Is Life', but the power chords that cemented 'Hear Me Lord': the album's loftiest, yet most underappreciated anthem – as he embodied the type of prog performer who flip-flops from chamber pop to aggressive, angular metal in the space of a few bars. As with 'My Sweet Lord', the song is notable for focusing on the influence of a higher power, and not on the all-consuming power that rests in their hands. 'Hear Me Lord' is, honest to God, an incredible song.

Lennon popped in, offering his seal of approval for the music he was exposed to. It's easy to imagine him contributing to the record, but there's no way McCartney would've been invited. As it happened, the bassist had sufficiently recovered from an alcoholic haze to prepare himself for the most difficult decision of his professional life. The decision to dissolve The Beatles partnership was not one McCartney took lightly, but he recognised the value of their combined wealth. The pain of losing three friends was mild compared to the loss of their life's earnings: 'I was just trying to walk away from them and keep it low-key, but I couldn't. I knew I had to do it. It was either that or letting Klein have the whole thing: all the fortune we'd worked for all our lives since we were children'.

Readying himself for the inevitable divorce, McCartney was armed with the paperwork and patience needed to win in court. His venom was aimed at Klein, who still represented the three other Beatles, and although McCartney understood that the action would blacken his name with the public at large, he nonetheless felt he had to bring Klein to court. He was still carrying the scars when he broached the subject with *GQ* in 2020: 'If I hadn't done that, it would have all belonged to Allen Klein. The only way I was given to get us out of that was to do what I did. I said, 'Well, I'll sue Allen Klein', and I was told I couldn't because he wasn't party to it: 'You've got to sue The Beatles''.

Stepping out of The Beatles might've seemed like a liberating proposition for Harrison, but he was slowly beginning to realise that his relationship with Pattie Boyd was also falling off a precarious slope, from which divorce seemed like the only viable solution. Every marriage has its difficulties, and Boyd was willing to put up with some of her husband's proclivities if it meant bringing them closer together in the long run. Deep down, she understood that he was seeking resolution, especially considering his upbringing, and she could definitely sympathise with his desire for enlightenment after experiencing so much loss in recent years. But her patience could only go so far, and she ached to return to her modelling career against Harrison's wishes. Unlike the other Beatles, their marriage had not produced any children, and the pair found themselves drifting with every passing day. It didn't help that Boyd's list of potential suitors was growing, and Clapton – effectively Harrison's musical lieutenant in 1970 – was struggling to keep whatever feelings he had, to himself. Clapton later admitted, 'I also coveted Pattie because she belonged to a powerful man who seemed to have everything I wanted: amazing cars, an incredible career and a beautiful wife'.

Released in November 1970, *All Things Must Pass* was something of an artistic triumph for the ex-Beatle, proving that music could be truthful and commercial in equal measure. The reviews were laudatory – *Billboard* thought it 'a masterful blend of rock and piety'; NME declared it 'music of the mind', and *Rolling Stone* commended the set as an 'extravaganza of piety and sacrifice and joy, whose sheer magnitude and ambition may dub it the *War and Peace* of rock 'n' roll'.

Briefly, Harrison could luxuriate in the critical acclaim that had once been Dylan's domain, and *All Things Must Pass* continues to inspire younger songwriters 50 years after its release. Oasis singer Liam Gallagher considers it his favourite of the solo Beatle albums, and Eurythmics songwriter and dobro enthusiast Dave Stewart has also sung the album's praises. Stewart told *CultureSonar*: 'I remember when George Harrison's *All Things Must Pass* came out, and thinking it was outstanding. He managed to bring out a pure tone with a thick glass slide. Beautiful tone. There are slide players out there who can play, but you can't always make them out. But you can always make out George'

1971: The First Live Aid?

By 1971, audience expectations of George Harrison might have risen to the near-Messianic heights he'd spent much of the 1960s ridiculing. It wasn't simply that he'd released the most warmly-received solo album of the four Beatles – indeed, after years of curtailing his ideas for the sake of a band he'd expressed disinterest in, bringing such a textured work to fruition, struck the music press as something of a victory. While the guitarist himself had shown disinterest in the praise at his feet, the critical applause must have aided him as he sailed down his own personal trajectory. And when tasked with a challenge set by the mentor that had ignited his interest in Eastern music, Harrison threw himself into the project with diligence, duty and goodwill. The ensuing Concert For Bangladesh not only set the blueprint for the charity rock spectacles Rock For Kampuchea and Live Aid, but it might just be the most rewarding thing Harrison committed to tape.

He could've done anything, but he decided he wanted to work with other artists, doubling as a writer and a guitar player. Harrison spent much of his creative energy focussing on Ronnie Spector's comeback album. His decision to work with the singer made practical sense, not least because his relationship with her husband remained fruitful. Moreover, Harrison was growing as a songwriter, and the prospect of writing songs for other artists only increased his artistic caché. Not only that, Phil Spector was growing more anxious: 'Phil wants a hit record with Ronnie again more than anything in the world', noted publisher Paul Case. 'I think he'd give up all his worldly possessions for that'. Invariably, Ronnie Spector didn't finish the album, although she did release 'Try Some, Buy Some': a startling number laced with a haunting lead vocal (Harrison was clearly happy with the arrangement, as he would use it himself on *Living In The Material World*. Sadly, his vocal doesn't have the power of the 1971 original).

Sitarist Ravi Shankar had known Harrison since the mid-1960s and had opened a portal for the guitar player that he never knew had existed. 'Ravi was my link into the Vedic world', Harrison explained. 'Ravi plugged me into the whole of reality. I mean, I met Elvis – Elvis impressed me when I was a kid, and impressed me when I met him because of the buzz of meeting Elvis, but you couldn't, later on, go-'round to him and say, 'Elvis, what's happening in the universe?''.

Harrison and Shankar met up regularly, combining their love of Indian music with a shared desire to enrich the more-wayward aspects of their souls. But for once, Shankar had sad news to offer the guitarist, as he was perturbed by the stories he heard of hungry refugees – millions of them – desperately searching for homes, following the Bangladesh Liberation War. Shankar recalled, 'I was in a very sad mood, having read all this news, and I said, 'George, this is the situation, I know it doesn't concern you, I know you can't possibly identify'. But while I talked to George, he was very deeply moved'.

Harrison valued Shankar's companionship, especially since his passages to India had brought solace to the guitarist's life, as The Beatles battled an ongoing cycle of album deadlines and setlists. So it was inevitable that once Shankar visited the guitar player with a suggestion, he would accept, and when Shankar suggested that the concert hold grander appeal than the typical rock gig, Harrison rose to the challenge and called up the biggest names in the business. The only question that remained for the critically acclaimed and commercially successful solo artist was whether or not he could piece together a night of rock altruism without deviating from the message in question.

Such was the importance of the event that Harrison even considered reforming The Beatles for the occasion, but Ringo Starr was the only one who turned up for the performances. Paul McCartney declined his invitation, which can't have surprised anyone considering their recent history, but John Lennon was a curious non-appearance, especially considering the support Harrison had offered him on 'Instant Karma'. It later transpired that Lennon declined his invitation because it precluded Yoko Ono from performing with him, but, in an interview, he chose not to mention that. Instead, Lennon offered a more-flimsy reason – he was holidaying in the Virgin Islands and didn't fancy flying in and out of New York as he did so. Seemingly, even he didn't seem interested in giving peace a chance if it meant disturbing his leisure time!

Given that Harrison had performed on Lennon's second album *Imagine*, it was strange to see a proud activist choosing this moment to absent themselves from a benefit concert. It probably didn't do much for their friendship. However, a key factor in the rapprochement between Lennon and Harrison was the fact that the former had always had great faith in the latter's abilities as a guitar player. While George Martin and Paul McCartney were guilty of under-nurturing Harrison's abilities, Lennon had always recognised his guitar style as one he could work with, and the pair had woven their guitars together on such songs as 'Yer Blues' and 'I Want You (She's So Heavy)'. Not that Lennon was always keen to return the favour – as early as 1968, he stopped contributing to Harrison's material, and whatever failings McCartney may have possessed, he was always willing to play bass when it was called for.

If Harrison held out hope that Lennon might return the gesture and play on one of his tracks, he was to be disappointed. But the *Imagine* album boasts some of Harrison's most magnetic guitar performances, many of them completed in a very short period. 'Gimme Some Truth' stemmed from the Beatles days, which likely accounts for the riveting instrumental section, as Harrison lurches forward and lets out a hypnotic guitar pattern that grows more sinister with every pressed string. Lennon loved the sound and credited the crunching effect to Harrison's 'steel finger'. Packing much of the rebellion that was heard on Lennon's excellent *Plastic Ono Band*, 'Gimme Some Truth' was ultimately wasted among a series of ill-thought-out compositions which earmarked the first of a trilogy of Lennon albums that did little to live up to his legend. By 1974 when Lennon had regained much of his creative mojo, Harrison was barely in his orbit, but they would work together again in 1973, this time completing a track for their beloved friend Ringo.

History has coloured Allen Klein a thug at best and a thief at worst, but there's no denying that the man was charismatic, self-confident and ambitious; not forgetting the fact that he won the respect of three Beatles at a pivotal time when each man was carving an identity outside the Beatles' orbit. 'No matter what everyone says, he's fair', Starr said of Klein. 'He doesn't want to shit on anyone, really'. Lennon, too, was quick to sing Klein's praises at the time: 'I love him, you know. I mean, he really has made me secure enough. I do have money for the first time really...'. There was more money to be found in The Beatle vaults, but it would be a while before they could lay their hands on it: not until their dissolution was formalised in December 1974.

While McCartney had his issues with *Let It Be*, his bandmates were satisfied with the record, and Harrison felt confident enough in his manager's abilities to organise the charity benefit concert. For now, his star was shining. But The Beatles were famously fickle with any affection they had for people who worked for them. Let's hope Klein enjoyed his stint in the spotlight because it didn't last.

Klein got the gears moving for what proved to be rock's noblest act of altruism. Something had to be done for Bangladesh, and at a time of great crisis, neither pride nor privilege had any place in what was a matter of life or death. Shankar hoped to raise 'maybe 25,000 dollars' for the

Bangladeshi refugees and victims of war, but Harrison thought they could do better than that: 'For a date, we had picked a period during which it had to be done. An Indian astrologer had said, 'this is a good period,' and he gave me around the beginning of August, and then we found the right day in August, and that was when Madison Square Garden was free, and so we rented it and did the show then'. Rehearsals began on 26 July, before Harrison, Shankar and Klein converged to give a press conference the following day. Klaus Voorman was there from the beginning, Badfinger were showing their support, and drummer Ringo Starr was due to fly in on 29 July. With Leon Russell and Billy Preston set to perform, Harrison had elicited enough big names to garner interest in the gig, but 'Bangla Desh' – released in the US and UK in the days before the concert – was there to remind audiences that the occasion wasn't altogether a very happy one:

My friend came to me with sadness in his eyes
Told me that he wanted help before his country dies
Although I couldn't feel the pain, I knew I had to try
Now I'm asking all of you to help us save some lives

Harrison was still new to success when he decided to organise the charity concert, and fuelled by the occasion, he realised this was the perfect opportunity to put aside his anger and perform three Beatles compositions amidst a smattering of recently-released solo numbers. No one was surprised to hear 'My Sweet Lord' among the songs, but 'Awaiting On You All' was a more-surprising choice, not least because of the incendiary rejoinders aimed towards the Pope. Considering the nature of the event, it seemed odd to alienate any potential Catholic punters, but cemented under the weight of the metallic riff, the song got an immediate response, and if the sentiment offended anyone, the wailing riff softened it.

Harrison was an able guitarist and could hold his own on a vocal or two. But unlike McCartney, Harrison had not fashioned a vocal style that could withstand a two-hour concert. It suited him to sing a tidy selection of his own work before passing the mantle to another singer while Harrison focused on the fretboard. Everywhere he played, his guitar sounded strong and sizzling, chugging through the songs like an adolescent experiencing their first joys of freedom in a world free from parents and regulations. But there was something grander to the guitar-playing as he found himself leading the charge for the first time on a live stage. From the opening jingle-jangle ring of 'Wah-Wah' to the closing 'Bangla Desh', Harrison attended to every performance as if his life – like the children he sang for – depended on it.

It was important that people attend the concert, but it was more important that the audience acknowledge the importance of the event and reflect on their own good fortune when it was robbed from so many others. Compromise was essential, but everyone did as they were asked, and with good humour too – when Harrison asked drummer Mike Gibbins if it was alright to play on a smaller set, he replied, 'I'm only here for the beer'.

Just because the concert stemmed from tragedy didn't mean the night had to be a forlorn one. It was essential that audiences enjoy the spectacle – because it was definitely spectacular – so Harrison's response was to affect a more companionable persona, even if it was just for one night. Between speeches, he could deliver note-perfect performances of 'Something' and 'Jumpin' Jack Flash', so he wisely chose to keep his comments brief and to the point. 'A couple of numbers from Leon', he said – his guitar foisted over his neck, his fingers preparing themselves for the choppy riff. At one point, you can catch Harrison on screen, the etchings of a smile emerging during the rendition of 'Young Blood'. Bolstered by Leon Russell's inimitable vocal style, Harrison slotted in nicely, chiming away at the blues number. (Saul Swimmer's footage was released in 1972, and the film offers a clear, unvarnished snapshot of the occasion.)

Harrison already had a design for the concert, having witnessed the way Brian Epstein operated. From topping the bill on *The Ed Sullivan Show* to fine-tuning a concept album based on vaudeville acts from the 1920s, everything the band did was big in scope and ambition. Shankar was humble enough to recognise the importance of rock, and Harrison felt that a stint at Madison Square Garden would drum up enough money to provide for the citizens of Bangladesh. It was perhaps just as well that Lennon declined to perform, as his ego, exuberance and predilection for the avant-garde was not in keeping with the humility, goodwill and general sense of camaraderie that went into the evening. Unlike Lennon, Harrison had shown disinterest in the avant-garde scene, summarising his scepticism with the salty, 'Avant-garde a clue'. Age did little to weather his disinterest in the field, and in 1996, The Beatles outfit declined to issue 'Carnival Of Light' – a much-rumoured ambient soundscape recorded three decades earlier – to the public, purportedly at Harrison's insistence.

As it happens, the evening's success had little to do with Harrison's connection to The Beatles. Even with the ever-reliable Starr on drums, the concert's enduring popularity had more to do with the *occasion* than with the torchbearers on the stage. 'It was obviously a very successful show', Harrison remembered. 'At the time when I was putting it together, I had no idea about how it was going to turn out. We were fortunate that it turned out well, but, at the same time, I had no idea about what I was letting myself in for. I had a vague idea, but it was all so much bigger than I thought'.

For Beatle fans, Harrison performed 'While My Guitar Gently Weeps', 'Something' and 'Here Comes The Sun': work generally regarded as his most beloved with the group. With Beatle associates Joey Molland and Klaus Voorman beside him, with Starr playing the part as drummer, Harrison had a strong backing for the night: providing some comfort for the man aching for Bob Dylan to appear on the night. Loath to appear in public since his motorcycle accident in 1966, Dylan nonetheless expressed an interest in performing at the event, but committing to the issue proved to be spottier. Unsure if his hero would appear, Harrison wrote 'Bob-?' in his handwritten setlist.

Similarly, Harrison was eager for Eric Clapton to play and booked several flights for him in the week leading up to the concert. Like Dylan, Clapton had become something of a rock recluse, leading some to believe he was dabbling freely in heroin. His newest band, Derek and the Dominos, had produced only one album, but it did at least feature the sizzling, up-tempo 'Layla' among its tracks. Much to her embarrassment, Pattie Boyd had served as the song's muse, but she was later blown away by the sincerity of the rocker: 'He's such an incredible musician that he's able to put his emotions into music in such a way that the audience can feel it instinctively. It goes right through you'.

As it happened, the erstwhile Cream guitarist appeared at the concert, having missed the majority of rehearsals, and Saul Swimmer's footage betrays a tired Clapton, looking older than his 26 years. But whatever demons were surfacing in his head, they did little to deminish the music, and his solos – particularly on the blinding 'While My Guitar Gently Weeps' – were exhilarating in their design.

Shortly before the concert, Harrison had begun working with Badfinger on their album *No Dice*, and in typical fashion, was working closely on their arrangements. 'George always encouraged Badfinger to harmonise', guitarist Joey Molland informed this writer in 2020. 'He got us to practice together and record together. That was the way it was done in those days. ... I mean, we could have recorded the voices separately: there was 24-track, 16-track. But George wouldn't let us; he made us sing together live. I think we sounded better because of it. The Beatles, they could harmonise'.

Harrison was clearly enjoying working with the band pegged by many as the next Beatles, but ultimately he had to bow out to focus on the charity concert. As it happens, Harrison bumped into burgeoning songwriter Todd Rundgren in New York, and the Pennsylvania-born musician agreed to complete the Badfinger sessions. Both men were credited on the final pressing, albeit with some reluctance from Rundgren, who later revealed, '(Harrison) didn't finish any of the songs, though he was perfectly willing to take the credit for the songs that I finished'.

Like XTC's Andy Partridge was to years later, Badfinger found Rundgren overbearing, and some of their original vision was lost in the process. But no matter how they felt about the album, nothing was going to stop them from performing with Harrison at Madison Square. It was the chance of a lifetime and a baptism of fire. Burgeoning songwriters Badfinger were on the cusp of a wave of success, and the opportunity to perform beside Harrison only helped to further their exposure. Lead guitarist Pete Ham joined Harrison for a jaunty rendition of 'Here Comes The Sun', which struck some in the music press as a passing of the torch from one British pop band to another. Though Badfinger's work was admirable – often spectacular – it scarcely translated into album sales, and sadly, their fortunes took a turn for the worse later in the 1970s. Ham died in 1975, and bassist Tom Evans similarly passed away in 1983. But rather than dwell on the tragedy, Badfinger should be commended for the way they shaped 1970s pop, and their contributions to the overarching sound of The Concert for Bangladesh, cannot be overlooked.

But no one present was a stranger to playing as part of an ensemble, and they certainly enjoyed singing together, as evinced by a particularly boisterous rendition of 'Awaiting On You All'. And as master of vocal arrangements, Harrison could go from performing a series of blinding harmonies, to singing a pastoral-tinted song virtually alone. Beyond that, Harrison excelled in a group format – as long as he was given free rein to play as he liked – and the concert boasts many of his most noteworthy guitar performances, both as a rhythm player and in his more traditional role on lead.

Yet for all the rock posturings that occurred during the night, it was Ravi Shankar's slow, hypnotic sitar installation 'Bangla Dhun' that held up best to relistening. Detached from the concert, it sounds like the work of a master instrumentalist performing an astonishingly-visceral piece. But by putting it first, it granted audience members permission to flow on their personal wayward spiritual search before being brought back to earth to the hits that made up their personal record collection.

Listening to the sitar suite in 2021, it holds up exceptionally well, offering the album a timelessness the turbocharged rock numbers did not. Best of all, it spoke wonders about the power of Shankar's presence over Harrison that he granted Shankar so much time and leeway on stage. Harrison was naturally stylish (Look how much more comfortable he looks in his Shea jacket compared to John Lennon), and frequently adorned himself in some of the wildest albeit sharpest suits of the 1960s. Being married to a model, Harrison was familiar with the latest sartorial trends, and his slim, sylph-like figure only helped to sell his outfit to the public. And so, he justly appeared dressed in a white suit and orange shirt, typifying an elegance that was neither ornate nor too casual but signalled him out as the leader of the night. But behind that boyish smile and holistic – even hippie-like – beard, was a man who was worried how the night would turn out. And yet Harrison may have surprised himself by the magnitude of the event: 'I knew The Beatles could always have a sellout, but on my own, it was different. We advertised for one concert, and they had to sell the tickets from midnight. The police came because it was such a big queue, and the police said they had to open the box office and sell the tickets from midnight, and they sold out by 5 a.m.'.

Although buoyed by excitement for the concert, Harrison nearly missed out on performing. It sounds inconceivable now, but it very nearly happened: 'My plane got caught in a violent thunderstorm and was struck three times by lightning', he recalled. 'We started bouncing around, dropping hundreds of feet all the time, and the lights went out. There were explosions and everybody was terrified. A Boeing 707 went over the top of us, missing us by inches'. Comforting himself in the chants he'd learned from the Krishna movement, Harrison called out for the hand of a higher being to bring them to safety. And so they landed, two hours after they were supposed to, leading the dazzled songwriter to believe that the chanting made the difference. It's tempting to think that this brush with death fashioned his resolve to finish the concert with the startling 'Bangla Desh', and to reiterate the value of life above all else in this world.

Purportedly written in ten minutes at a piano, 'Bangla Desh' was a gut-punch rocker, cautioning listeners against the consequences of their ignorance. Interestingly, it mirrored Bob Geldof's approach to Live Aid fourteen years later. Disappointed by the British public's apathy towards the famine in Ethiopia, the Irish-born singer appeared on television and begged viewers all over the world to 'Give us as much money as we know you have'. (There's no need for us to print some of the swearing uttered by The Boomtown Rats frontman!)

The Concert for Bangladesh

Performers:

George Harrison: vocals, electric guitar, acoustic guitar

Bob Dylan: vocals, acoustic guitar, harmonica

Eric Clapton, Jesse Ed Davis: electric guitar

Don Preston: vocals, electric guitar

Pete Ham, Joey Molland: acoustic guitar

Tom Evans: 12-string acoustic guitar

Leon Russell: vocals, piano

Klaus Voormann, Carl Radle: bass

Ringo Starr: vocals, drums, tambourine

Billy Preston: vocals, Hammond organ

Jim Keltner: drums

Mike Gibbins: tambourine, maracas

Jim Horn, Jackie Kelso, Allan Beutler: saxophone

Chuck Findley, Ollie Mitchell: trumpet

Lou McCreary: trombone

Claudia Lennear, Joe Greene, Jeanie Greene, Marlin Greene, Dolores Hall, Don Nix, Don Preston: vocals, percussion

Ravi Shankar: sitar

Ali Akbar Khan: sarod

Alla Rakha: tabla

Kamala Chakravarty: tambura

Record label: Apple

Recorded 1 August 1971, Live at Madison Square Garden, New York

Produced by George Harrison and Phil Spector

Release dates: UK: 10 January 1972, US: 20 December 1971

Chart placings: UK: 1, US: 2

Running Time: 99:32

The men were ready to get out there and sing, although one or two of the performers were growing visibly anxious due to the size of the crowd.

'I was crazy with nerves beforehand', Starr confessed. 'But if you have done your job, it's okay. You soon relax. It was nice anyway because we had a lot of good pals around. Bob was as nervous as anybody that night. We weren't out just to entertain each other. We wanted to entertain the 25,000 people who had paid to come in. It is no good just standing there with your guitar and freaking yourself out'. Ultimately, the drummer forgot some of the words to 'It Don't Come Easy', but he was supported by a pummelling brass section, and the performance has a punch that's even more rollicking than the single itself. (Though credited to Starr alone, the track was produced by Harrison, and he probably had a hand in writing it too.)

Judging by the audience's reaction, they were too excited watching two Beatles singing together to notice a minor hiccup, and Starr could enjoy the moment knowing that he single-handedly kept a remarkable rhythm while singing the number. And, of course, at the other extreme, no one sang with as much vibrancy as Dylan, who somehow managed to perform five of his own songs without detracting from Harrison or the event in question. From 'A Hard Rain's Gonna Fall' to 'Just Like A Woman', Dylan's material soared over the audience; the applause thunderous, the enthusiasm ecstatic. And then there was Harrison, clearly relishing the moment to perform beside his idol, inspiration and friend.

Another great moment in the film comes when Dylan sings the opening verse to 'It Takes A Lot To Laugh, It Takes A Train To Cry'. As Dylan carries on, we hear the sound of a quirky guitar entering, lacing itself over the offbeat rhythm. Clearly comfortable in himself, Dylan lets out a ferocious roar, exhibiting a wildness that had scarcely made it onto his studio work. A large chunk of the song is dedicated to the instrumental sections, and even Dylan joins in the fun: his lips pursed firmly on the harmonica. Wailing into the microphone, Dylan reverts back to the lyrics, his voice bursting with joy on the verses.

Famously the least showbizzy of The Beatles, Harrison nonetheless possessed a desire to explore new challenges and see them out to their fullest potential. 'George had a really curious mind, and when he got into something, he wanted to know everything', recalled Olivia Harrison as she was promoting the Martin Scorsese film *George Harrison: Living in the Material World*. 'He had a crazy side too. He liked to have fun, you know'. Ultimately, that's what made The Concert for Bangladesh the memorable occasion that it was. The aims were far-reaching, the music endearing. But taking the event seriously was not the same as the musicians taking themselves too seriously, and with Harrison as their captain, the crew followed in line.

Harrison arrives onstage before plugging into the opening bars of 'Wah-Wah'. There's a hesitancy to his voice, but none on his guitar, and the lacerating riff powers with a wildness a mere shade away from heavy metal. At the close of the song, Harrison turns to more folk-oriented territory, and he starts playing 'My Sweet Lord''s opening lines. Flatter than the record, the performance is bolstered by a committed vocal, and any nerves felt on the rollicking predecessor are quickly discarded. Then there's 'Awaiting On You All' – bursting with passion, and Harrison relishes the chance to poke fun at the Pope that spearheads the world's most popular religion. By then, the audiences were clapping along with Billy Preston: fuelling the keyboardists' gospel ballad with the spark he needed to burn off of. Channelling the atmosphere, Preston's 'That's The Way God Planned It', soars with spontaneity, style and soul; Harrison's guitar ripping along to every word that falls from Preston's mouth. Swinging to the music, Preston jumps up from his stool, and Harrison cackles knowingly, both relishing the moment. Before The Concert for Bangladesh, Harrison held a secondary position in the ranks of rock hierarchy. His songs, silhouettes and guitar stylings were the workings of a craftsman, not an artist. He seemed happy to stand in the background while the flashier members of The Beatles entourage stepped forward to sign autographs and speak into the microphone. The Concert for Bangladesh changed all that. Suddenly it was Harrison who emerged as one of the world's most formidable talents, and the concert is still referenced in interviews by people who want to pull off an event of a similar scale.

The film was released in 1972, but by then, the atmosphere had changed significantly, and Harrison found himself dealing with the very people he had tried to avoid speaking to by becoming a guitar player. Unlike Lennon's more impractical 'bed-in' practice, Harrison's ambitions were more attainable and realistic. But rather than face the ire of the world press, he was forced to overcome an obstacle that threatened to ruin the integrity of the concerts. Having neglected to apply to the US government for tax-exempt status, Harrison and Klein were informed that the proceeds were liable to tax. Britain was also proving to be difficult, and not even a meeting with the Financial Secretary to the Treasury could sway Patrick Jenkin from *scrubbing* the purchase of tax on the record. When the album (another triple-set) was released in the United Kingdom, it was unusually expensive for a casual music buyer (in other words, the record's intended audience), partially because of the government's refusal to waive its tax surcharge. Given his desire to send as much money to the starving people in Bangladesh, Harrison was growing understandably agitated, and he no longer felt any desire to keep it a secret.

While the performances were jaunty and lively, it was getting harder and harder to release these vignettes to the world at large. There were reports emerging as early as 23 August 1971 that the live album had been delayed due to 'legal issues'. Considering that the goal of The Concert for Bangladesh was to create money for people in need, Harrison was understandably anxious to see it shipped to the right country. Klein had neglected to apply in advance to the US government to be given tax-exempt status for the concerts, which meant much of the concert earnings had to be siphoned off. Politics, as ever, emerged behind the scenes – EMI/Capitol and Columbia/CBS felt they had a rightful claim to issue the album and worked on maintaining their business interests. EMI chairman Bhaskar Menon was also reluctant to acquiesce and lower the labels fees, even though none of the luminaries who performed at the event were paid for it. During his appearance on *The Dick Cavett Show*, Harrison took the opportunity to slam the chairman: 'I mean, I'll just put it out with CBS and, you know, Bhaskar will have to sue me. (raises fist) Bhaskar Menon!'

Ultimately, Columbia was given tape distribution rights in North America and earned 25 cents from every copy sold. The experience left a sour taste in Harrison's mouth – a feeling of disgust that he would experience once more in later years as he stood up to defend the plagiarism accusations against 'My Sweet Lord' in open court. The moment was slipping away, and Harrison was anxious that the album be released before Christmas. Like the concert, no one was getting paid royalties, and Harrison was growing impatient with what he perceived as shameless profiteering on the part of the record companies. His appearance had a functional and emotional impact on the world's viewers, and critics sided with Harrison against what was commonly regarded as an uncharitable move. Having dedicated much of his time to organising the event, the musician was now spending more of his spare time overlooking the edit of the footage and working on the album mix.

Producer Phil Spector was more tricky to track down, and even when he was there to work, he was acting less professionally than he used to. 'Phil was at the concert, dancing in the front when it was being recorded',

Harrison retorted, crediting Gary Kellgren with what he considered to be the album's key work. By the time Harrison was ready to complete the follow up to *All Things Must Pass*, he decided it was easier to produce it himself than to wait fruitlessly for Spector to show up.

Creating the role of *rock saviour* has long been a preoccupation of the music industry, especially when it comes to raising funds for famine relief. While a rock star may take pleasure from their charitable endeavours, too often, they find their honourable intentions are undermined by external circumstances. In an effort to quash pirate copies from being sold, posters were placed in record shops that read, 'Save a starving child. Don't buy a bootleg!'. It was a strangely-corporate approach, especially when it came off the back of a gig-based on community and benevolence. Yet the statements were symptomatic of a wider feeling that rock musicians were there to serve the money men, and the spirit that had lit the 1960s was beginning to dwindle now that the accountants were purportedly dictating terms. Rock was supposed to be a voice for the young and aspiring, but it was growing harder to champion a movement that was becoming more mechanical with every passing day. One can't help but sympathise with Harrison – arguably the least business-oriented of The Beatles, and certainly the most unorthodox, at least from a Western point of view – as he was becoming more entrenched in a world he was eager to consign to the breakup of The Beatles.

Finally, the album was released on 20 December 1971, just in time for the Christmas market. Christmas is traditionally a time of goodwill, and buyers were no doubt deeply moved by the portrait of a malnourished child looking solemnly over an empty bowl. Journalist Mick Farren declared it 'the greatest achievement ever by its organisers – a group headed by George Harrison, Ravi Shankar and Allen Klein'.

Having exerted so much of himself for a debut album and a triumphant and arguably game-changing spectacle of rock philanthropy, Harrison now needed a break, and spent much of 1972 in silent recuperation. In the meantime, he cannily opted to install a 16-track recording studio in Friar's Park. Ensconced in a guest suite, the studio – like most things in Harrison's life – was built for work and pleasure, and the guitarist now felt even more comfortable in his home now that it doubled as his office. But behind his locked doors stood a man as determined as ever to blaze a new pathway for himself, but it was one he would soon have to walk as an unmarried man. Having crashed his Mercedes, the Liverpool-born musician was suspended from driving for much of the year. He was a confident driver and, thankfully, emerged largely unscathed, although Boyd – sitting in the passenger seat – was more badly injured, which can't have helped his credentials as a husband in a marriage that had been rocky for some time.

Harrison was keenly aware of the ways in which his role as a charity entrepreneur might be put to good use as a political figure. He encouraged the virtues of meditation, he espoused the works of the Krsna movement, and he warned listeners of the horrors of the war waging in Bangladesh. Violence disgusted him, no matter what the presentation, and not even the shootings in Derry could compel him to champion the Irish Republican Movement. Like McCartney, Harrison's mother held strong ties to Ireland, and like Lennon, Harrison could be compelled into action to write a polemical anthem, regardless of the public interest. Lennon spoke up and included two urgent numbers – 'The Luck Of The Irish' and 'Sunday Bloody Sunday' – on the otherwise underwhelming *Some Time In New York City*, while Mccartney went one further, demanding that Wings write a single in response to the killings. Within two days of Bloody Sunday, McCartney's punchy 'Give Ireland Back To The Irish' made it onto the airwaves, only for the BBC to ban it. Fittingly, the single hit the number-1 spot in Ireland, as it did in Spain, proving that there was an appetite for work of a rebellious nature outside of the United Kingdom. But Harrison had little interest in such a market and actively avoided saluting a movement that didn't express themselves through peace, promise and mindfulness.

By the end of the 1970s, Harrison indirectly picked up a film that revolved around the IRA's hold over London. *The Long Good Friday* – complete with a magnetic lead from Bob Hoskins – stands amongst the best work Handmade Films produced, though the guitarist himself found the project difficult to sit through. Hoskins admitted in the 1980s: 'I've actually spoken to George about *The Long Good Friday*. He said, 'If I'd have known it was that violent, I wouldn't have taken it on''.

Harrison was writing in his spare time, but he wasn't in a hurry to record another album, and he certainly wasn't going to write one in a last-minute attempt to further his fame. 'I wouldn't really care if no one ever heard of me again', he told *Record Mirror*. 'I just want to play and make records and work on musical ideas'. This wasn't some sort of bullish posture on Harrison's part: he was happier in his house than he was onstage. Nevertheless, he did perform on other people's records; this time cloaked as a session player. In the spring of 1972, he contributed a guitar solo to Harry Nilsson's biting 'You're Breaking My Heart' – a terse rocker that demonstrated the American vocalist's fury over the demise of his marriage, through a series of fiery epithets. Unlike Lennon's more desperate use of profanity, 'You're Breaking My Heart' was a treatise on despair that utilised the F word with venom and vigour. The boisterous song – one of Nilsson's more-exhilarating – featured on *Son of Schmilsson*: an album that incidentally featured Ringo Starr and Klaus Voorman as rhythm section. And then there was Peter Frampton – rocking into the music with gusto, his star soon to rise to stratospheric heights.

More happily, Harrison could finally bask in his achievements, knowing that he'd shown the world its potential for magnanimity at the turn of a more uncertain decade. The way the finances were handled was undoubtedly a blow and likely put a dampener on any good spirits he'd had after the concert. But hopeful as ever, he turned to meditation to guide him through the duress. The recordings still hold up, not just for their nobility but for the standard of performance. Every guitar hook was played proficiently, every note was sung honestly, and every man was happy to be there. Such was its power that the album set *The Concert For Bangladesh* won Album of the Year at the Grammy Awards in March 1973. It was a deserved victory, and likely helped Harrison regain his confidence as he started work on his sophomore studio album. Recognising the importance of the event, he decided to focus on the many positives, and whatever negatives projected themselves onto him, would lessen over the years. As well he should have: it's hard to imagine any other celebrity – let alone a Beatle – showing such initiative, particularly at such a critical juncture in their solo career. But in many ways, the concert was more than a noble gesture: it was a deeply personal one. Altruistically, Paul McCartney saluted Harrison in 1985 when the bassist was interviewed at Live Aid, and the guitarist too came to a similar resolution as the concert celebrated its 20th anniversary: 'The money we raised was secondary. What we did was show that musicians and people are more humane than politicians'. And Shankar? He echoed Harrison's view: 'What happened is now history. It was one of the most moving and intense musical experiences of the century'.

1973: When He Was Fab

Almost ten years since the Beatles exuberant appearance on *The Ed Sullivan Show*, George Harrison's *Living In The Material World* album was released. In contrast to the spirited showcase that welcomed America from the doldrums of a post-Kennedy slumber, *Material World* demonstrated a slower, more detached persona aching for meaning in a world that seemed determined to lose it. Where once Harrison stood in between two genius songwriters – his voice tipping their harmonies to the foremost of their most infectious energy – he now stood as a wiser, more thoughtful artist essaying aphorisms, mantras and philosophies even more far-reaching than the elegies heard on Pete Townsend's searching, soulful albums.

Harrison's favourite Beatles album was *Rubber Soul*, which made sense considering his guitar work was a mixture of rock and blues brought to life by a swagger that was his alone. Clearly, he was uninterested in ornamentation, and even as late as 1987, felt apathy towards *Sgt. Peppers Lonely Hearts Club Band*: nominally considered their most fertile work. It's hard to find another band with as much staying-power as the Liverpool quartet; therefore, it was easier to see them in the realm of cinema, which was fitting, considering how neatly they strode across the screen on *A Hard Day's Night*.

The Beatles influence over pop culture was comparable to that of James Bond, and every member of the band represented one of the many custodians who has helped steer the franchise in its near-60-year history. The doe-eyed Paul McCartney (who composed the magnificent theme for *Live and Let Die*) had an insouciant nature that was comparable to Roger Moore's, while John Lennon (tortured, tempered and frequently reluctant to acquiesce to the trappings of stardom) slots in nicely as the Daniel Craig character. Affable, good-natured and decidedly undervalued by the press – Ringo Starr bore much in common with Meath icon Pierce Brosnan, which leaves George Harrison as the Timothy Dalton of The Beatles. Both Dalton and Harrison were wrongly-perceived as 'quiet' by members of the press (overlooking the thoughtful and nuanced interviews they granted), and then there was their supposed dourness: an opinion that neglected the fact that both men contained a wickedly-dark sense of humour. Finally, there is the matter of their second entries (Dalton's *Licence to Kill* and Harrison's *Living In The Material World*): thoughtful exercises in penitence that followed in the footsteps of two more flashy debuts. Like *Licence to Kill*, *Material World*'s critical stock has only increased in the decades since its release, and like that 1989 Bond entry that supposedly 'killed the franchise', Harrison's effort stemmed from a place of conceptual resonance and not commercial agenda – putting it crudely, it was his *farewell to arms*.

Like Dalton's Bond at the beginning of his movie, Harrison found himself feeling adrift from everything his peers expected of him. He was spending more time by himself, singing in his spare time, and holding onto a principle he valued much more than some hit written for a faceless audience he had no interest in acquiescing to. It's a strange metaphor, but if Harrison was a Bond, it wasn't the louche playboy journeying to space, or the burned-out poker player aching for another person to complete him – it was the erudite, introspective spy willing to walk away from fame for a more solitary path.

1973 was a year of great change for Harrison. Having extricated himself from Klein's services (McCartney gloated in an interview that he sensed the other three Beatles felt he was 'right' about the manager), Harrison was introduced to Denis O' Brien: an American attorney and friend of comedian and actor Peter Sellers. Helping Harrison wade through his tax returns, O'Brien enjoyed a stable relationship with the Beatle, and together they co-founded Handmade Films in 1979. 'The chairman of Shell, of RTZ, of IBM, of Ford', boasted O'Brien. 'I've met all these people, and I've never met anyone as together as George'.

Harrison was still contributing to other people's works, so anyone who felt uncomfortable with his epistolising, could happily listen to another record featuring his dynamic guitar contributions. Interestingly, he featured on one of the more-popular novelty records of 1973. Cheech & Chong hardly constituted a band; they hardly constituted a comedy duo, come to think of it. But like Monty Python before them, they too left an indelible stamp on pop culture, so it was only a matter of time before they started writing songs. Harrison and Klaus Voorman just happened to be in the same studio as the pair were writing the novelty number 'Basketball Jones Featuring Tyrone Shoelaces'. Harrison wound up playing guitar on the track, and while only the most perverse of fans would characterise the song as anything more than an experiment in sound, it does feature the guitarist embodying the sparkling power that so often typified a 1970s rock track. Much of the music of the era was becoming more docile, and many acts (especially those from Britain) were acquiescing to the demands that radio expected of them.

Pop music is rarely about authenticity but rather aims to capture the zeitgeist of the moment. Harrison was never a natural shoo-in for pop, but Ringo Starr – all baritone voice and jollity – slotted in with the icons of the era, and his anthems 'It Don't Come Easy' and 'Back Off Boogaloo' showed there was an appetite for punchy pop numbers, delivered under the drummer's trademark drawl. His first album, *Sentimental Journey* was poor, but *Beaucoup of Blues* was a decided improvement, and Starr was growing in confidence: every song delivered with gusto and general good wit. Compared to the darker work proffered by the other three solo Beatles, Starr's work was dependably frothy, inoffensive and charming. His third album *Ringo* – commonly regarded as his best – showcased a synthesis of ideas in keeping with the rise of glam and proto-punk. The synthesizer featured prominently on 'Six O'Clock': a jaunty McCartney ballad that would not have sounded out of place on the 1975 Wings masterwerk *Venus and Mars*. 'I'm The Greatest', with its thunderous riff and soaring chorus seemed more interested in the music of yesterday than the 1970s and presented Starr enjoying the fruits rock had gifted him. Written by John Lennon, the song presented something of a Beatle reunion, as it combined Starr's drumming, Lennon's kitschy piano and Harrison's belting guitar lick. McCartney – who worked with Starr elsewhere on the record – is absent from the track, though Klaus Voorman (eager as ever to work with the band he met in Hamburg) provides a bass line that sounds pleasantly Beatlesque. With the four Beatles performing, producing and writing, *Ringo* (1973) is the closest the band ever came to releasing a comeback record (the negligible 'Free As A Bird' scarcely counts, largely because it was cobbled from an unfinished recording that was more than a decade old), and it demonstrated a loyalty to the fan base who had followed the band from one decade into the next. Best of all, the album boasted a Harrison/Starr co-write, and 'Photograph' – an ode to lost love in the midst of great upset – provides Beatles listeners with the splendours of a writing partnership every bit as striking as the Lennon/McCartney prototype. With its purposeful guitar hook and explosive (even semi-Spector-like) production sound, the song remains an unabashed highlight in the drummer's solo canon. And in the wake of Harrison's death, the song took on a new meaning at the 2002 *Concert for George*, as Starr came face-to-face with the song's most revealing lyric: '...and I realise you're not coming back anymore'. Starr later paid a more-direct tribute to the guitarist with the bouncy 'Never Without You', but it lacked the raw nerve of the live performance. He enjoyed a close bond with Lennon, but Harrison was another close chum, and the drummer could always depend on Harrison to help out with his solo career. Starr benefitted from the collaboration in more ways than one: 'I only know three chords', he admitted, 'and he'd stick four more in, and they'd all think I was a genius'.

Living In The Material World

Personnel:
George Harrison: vocals, electric guitar, acoustic guitar, dobro, sitar
Nicky Hopkins: piano, electric piano
Gary Wright: organ, harmonium, electric piano, harpsichord
Klaus Voormann: bass, upright bass, tenor saxophone
Ringo Starr: drums
Jim Keltner: drums, percussion
Jim Horn: saxophone, flute
Zakir Hussain: tabla
Record label: Apple
Recorded February 1971, October 1972-March 1973, Apple, London; FPSHOT, Oxfordshire; Abbey Road, London.
Produced by George Harrison and Phil Spector
Release dates: UK: 22 June 1973, US: 30 May 1973
Charting placings: UK: 2, US: 1
Running Time: 43:55

In one way, *Living In The Material World* captures the songwriter more confidently than *All Things Must Pass* did. Without the many multitudes of instruments there to decorate the soundscape, the album's success now depended on Harrison's delivery, and it shows him singing with more flexibility and ease than previously. The Homeric 1970 triple-album had a lavish production design that helped to soften some of the more uncompromising edges. *Living In The Material World* held fewer flourishes, and Harrison was delving further into the realm of spiritual rock, and while the end result isn't as fresh or as pioneering-sounding, it's arguably the more honest effort; every song delivered with commitment to the crusade he was embarking on. His name was Harrison, George Harrison.

Harrison had always regarded Bob Dylan highly – both as a person and a songwriter – and like the freewheeling singer, Harrison never felt beholden to a direction his fans had set for him: 'It was all still pure

Dylan, and he has to find out his own directions', Harrison said. 'If he felt he wanted electrocution, that's the way he had to do it'. In one way, *Living In The Material World* showed a reverse Dylan – where *All Things Must Pass* had been boisterous and loud (not least because it was drenched in reverb), *Material World* was a much more stripped-back affair. Had it followed a similar template to its predecessor, it may well have been another monster hit, but the songs – written after *All Things Must Pass* – were disconnected from the more anthemic qualities of that album. As such, it was wiser to distance itself from the debut by creating a world that was unique to it alone. Klaus Voorman recalled: '*All Things Must Pass* might be better, but those songs are incredible. You can hear from the LP what his aim was; he definitely had a message he wanted to get across'.

In sharp contrast to *All Things Must Pass*'s colosseum of noise, *Living In The Material World* was a more sparse affair, culminating in a record that utilised a core trio of Klaus Voorman, Jim Keltner and Nicky Hopkins. Ringo Starr guested on a few tracks, but otherwise, there were few celebrity walk-ins. Whatever guitar solos were recorded tended to be brief, brittle, embellishments by Harrison's beautiful slide. As ever, Voorman enjoyed himself during the recording, but John Barham – who arranged many of the gorgeous orchestral moments on *All Things Must Pass* – saw a different side to the doctrinal Beatle: 'It was obvious to anyone who knew George, that he was seriously stressed. I think it was most likely the daunting task of attempting to match the extraordinary artistic and commercial success of *All Things Must Pass*. Added to that was the stress of litigation in connection with 'My Sweet Lord', and I believe George and Pattie were having problems in their relationship. They are not amongst my happiest memories of working with him. His stress – the causes of which I think I understand much better now than I did then – sometimes made him short-tempered and irritable. As orchestral arranger and music director working with session musicians at the time, I felt that George's stress was negatively affecting the working atmosphere in the studio'.

And yet, the album sounds calm, collected and completely at peace with itself. Starr's footwork made a reappearance on the unashamedly blues-sounding title track – he even got to perform a mini drum solo as his name was called out as one of the fixtures of the material world. Fame, it seemed, only furthered to distract man's true purpose in discovering the spiritual world that lay beyond the skies – a plane where man and woman weren't measured by their fortune but the purity of their soul.

Harrison summarised, 'the whole point to being here really, is to figure a way to get out'. Fans of Harrison could point to the album's sincerity, as the fables that had made up his first album were presented here without the dressing and pomposity that had laced it. But there's no denying that the album lacked braggadocio – bravado even – and the subtle, cerebral textures seemed to favour a different type of audience to those who had bought Harrison's records up to that point.

And then comes the title track – bristling with ambition and grandeur, the Indian textures bursting through, every note rushing to the forefront. The album's second out-and-out masterpiece ('Give Me Love (Give Me Peace On Earth)' was the first), the song is also the loudest expression of sound and did much to dispel rumours that he'd lost his nerve since becoming a solo artist.

> I got born into the material world
> Getting worn out in the material world
> Use my body like a car
> Taking me both near and far
> Met my friends all in the material world

'Living In The Material World' holds one of Harrison's most demanding vocals – rising from the rock textures that pepper the verses to something more fragile and ethereal on the bridge, his wailing falsetto gliding nicely over the mosaic of sitar, guitar and tabla that cement the track. Caught in the urgency of the track, Harrison acquiesces to the band and allows the saxophone to blare through the instrumental suite, the drums tumbling away as if playing along to a Led Zeppelin or Genesis track. Salvaging himself from the ruins with 'the Lord Sri Krishna's grace', Harrison rests from the vocal booth with just enough energy left to lead the band through a frantic fever-driven fade-out that tips its hat to the Elvis records of old. In 'Living In The Material World', it's possible to discern a sense of tension that was building in Harrison's head, but the tremendous – if troubled – work nonetheless knew that the best way to generate a sympathetic response from the public was to end on a jocular, playful note.

Almost every song on the album turned out to be a mantra of some kind, which is why the songs were best produced unadorned. In some cases, the barrelling drum patterns turned out to be advantageous for the listener since the roll of the toms vibrated over the more-serene chords.

The British magazines – still proud of their image as subversives and voices of the counterculture – reacted scathingly (*NME* called it 'so damn holy I could scream'), but 'The Lord Loves the One (That Loves the Lord)' was received better in America, with *Rolling Stone* even suggesting Aretha Franklin get '...her hands on it...'. This song, like the rest of the material, was an extension of his personality, and therefore, his commitment to God. He was chanting regularly, but this only served to extend the rift that was growing between him and some of his colleagues. Engineer Geoff Emerick recalled: 'George could be infuriating at times. Every now and then, he would get into this Hare Krishna thing, and he'd walk around with this little bag that resembled a sling...'. Ultimately, Emerick found it difficult to record Harrison's vocals whenever the singer found himself in such a stance: '...he'd start to answer you, but then begin mumbling away, chanting his mantra'. In what was swiftly becoming a tradition, Harrison countered these criticisms with an attack of his own. He told Melody Maker in 1971: 'They feel threatened when you talk about something that isn't just 'be-bop-a-lula', and if you say the words 'God' or 'Lord', it makes some people's hair curl'.

Living In The Material World was a brave step forward for an artist who could've offered the world another helping of *All Things Must Pass*. But he had to be true to himself and where his life was heading, and the idea of another densely-produced, dynamic guitar-inflected album, simply didn't appeal to him. Notwithstanding Spector's influence on 'Try Some Buy Some', *Living In The Material World* is otherwise a deeply cerebral album and one that benefits from repeat listenings. What it lacks in clarity, it makes up for in character, ably demonstrating the thoughts of a man embracing the trials his 30s were presenting him with. The songs are rich, beautifully-drawn parables that plunge headfirst into the inner psyche. Almost without exception, the compositions celebrate the environment that surrounds us, before wagging a finger at the businessmen determined to destroy it. Compared to Harrison's earlier efforts, the album sounded quaint and contemplative, but it was no less philosophical, and in many places, it was more profound.

Unfortunately, any sense of empathy had long dissipated on 'The Lord Loves The One (That Loves The Lord)' – a blistering gospel track, let down by a message that was overtly haughty, didactic and sanctimonious. The elegist who'd penned such thoughtful tracks as 'What Is Life' and 'Awaiting On You All' is nowhere to be found here, but rather reduced himself to slogans that would make a reverend groan in embarrassment:

The Lord loves the one that loves the Lord
And the law says if you don't give, then you don't get loving

The project had its roots in a cancelled Ronnie Spector album, and rather than re-record the backing to 'Try Some, Buy Some', Harrison simply put his vocal in place of hers. The original track had vigour, passion and presence, culminating in a mandolin-filled coda that may have inspired John Lennon to adopt a similar arrangement on 'Happy Xmas (War is Over)'. But Harrison's decision to release his own version of 'Try Some, Buy Some' struck many of his fans as curious, especially since it put him in direct competition with Ronnie Spector. And as a vocalist, he had none of her grit or raw, guttural power and ultimately sounded weedy against the many instruments blaring behind him. But, truthful as ever, he did sound sincere on the track, and it satiated listeners aching for a blaring rocker in the style of 'Awaiting On You All' or 'Isn't It A Pity'.

Harrison's reputation as the most philosophical Beatle would endure, not least because he treated *Living In The Material World* as his expression of spiritual intent. If he had any ambitions of returning to rock, this was not the album to prove it. 'Who Can See It' – the closest thing the album had to a rock tune – opens with a startling arpeggio, before Harrison's yearning vocal takes over and brings the track into more-interesting territories. Rather than write about a man searching for a woman, Harrison shows himself as a jailbird aching for forgiveness, even if he can't muster the strength to bring it on himself. Purportedly inspired by American tenor Mario Lanza, the song holds one of Harrison's most complicated vocals, and delivers an agony that could only have come from a place of emotional duress. Deeply personal, this confessional hymn showed his intent to live privately after a decade spent running in the spotlight. The recording was blotted slightly by a smouldering string section, but the vocal – hungry yet unhurried in its resolve – compensated for this oversight. It was a decided improvement on the risible 'Don't Let Me Wait Too Long', and showed that the largely-cryptic songwriter did have a beating heart. This was, after all, the elegist who had written such romantic fodder as 'Something' and 'Here Comes The Sun', so it shouldn't have come as much of a surprise that he was capable of writing from the heart. But he had a reputation for writing work that was intellectual, introspective and forward-thinking, which sat at odds with the rigours of pop in 1973.

By the time Harrison released *Living In The Material World*, it was apparent that he had little to no interest in the trends that were being spearheaded by *Top of the Pops*. Perhaps because of the way the guitars sparkled, Harrison was being reminded of the more facile groups he'd climbed the ladder to 1960s stardom with. His tastes were firmly set on more pastoral, acoustic textures, and though the genre was unquestionably American, his style of singing was unquestionably British in tone. Harrison's detachment from glam rock most likely stemmed from his resistance to ostentation and flash. He was, after all, a man of great honesty, and heralded the importance of truth above all else. And though David Bowie shared a similar desire for enlightenment – as he presented so beautifully on *Hunky Dory* – Harrison didn't seem too enamoured by the performer. Harrison recounted in a radio conversation with John Lennon: 'David Bowie ... these were my very words, and I hope he wasn't offended by it, because all I really meant was what I said. I pulled his hat up from over his eyes and said, 'Hi man, how are you, nice to meet you', pulled his hat up and said, you know, do you mind if I have a look at you, to see what you are because I've only ever seen those dopey pictures of you'. If Bowie was offended, he shouldn't have been – Harrison also thought the photos he'd seen of Elton John were similarly 'stupid'! (Bowie recorded a tasteful rendition of 'Try Some, Buy Some' in 2003, recognising his rendition as a personal parable, and one that applauded his recovery from addiction: '...but when I first heard the song in '74, I was yet to go through my heavy drug period', Bowie told Paul Du Noyer. 'And now it's about the consolation of having kicked all that and turning your life around'.)

We haven't looked at 'Give Me Love (Give Me Peace On Earth)': the album's most assured effort and Harrison's most successful single. In a career characterised by scripture and slide, Harrison rarely melded the two as tastefully as he did on this track. The slide positions the narrative before Nicky Hopkins' piano takes over, and the guitars fade to the sound of Harrison's chant. Then the slide returns, elevating the track to a hungrier, happier terrain, and the quest that glues the song now holds an urgency that's equal-parts sexual and spiritual. Ultimately, he releases himself from the 'heavy load', for a lighter future beyond the fretboard.

Some of his compositions had leaned too heavily on John Lennon's influence (not forgetting Bob Dylan's), but 'Give Me Love' could not have been written by anyone but Harrison, and the track – pure and simple as it is – transcends 'My Sweet Lord' for power, even if it didn't latch onto its popularity. Nevertheless, 'Give Me Love' was another monumental success and deservedly hit the UK top 10. Overseas, the single was more popular still, and it nested at the top of the US *Billboard* chart. But the juggernaut would soon jackknife, and Harrison spent the rest of the decade releasing albums to dwindling responses. If the *Living In The Material World* record put a dent in the public zeitgeist, it paled palpably to the trajectory his debut started, and this sophomore fatigue would hang over him for the rest of the decade.

Still, the record – a trim single album piggybacking off two monster triple records – also developed the spiritual themes in extremis: yearning, searching, and soulful, it illustrated the harder nature of spiritual practices. The characters in 'The Lord Loves The One (That Loves The Lord)' seem to be somewhat wracked; the prisoners of a self-inflicted judgement consumed by remorse and revelation. The drums – largely subdued on the record – emerge from the back to thunder away, driving the metaphor into the minds of an unknowing public. The last time Harrison had been so haughty, had been on 'Within You Without You', but the *Sgt. Pepper* standout – beautifully designed through sitar, strings and silhouettes – stood amongst a series of more jaunty vignettes that made the track more palatable for agnostics. But 'The Lord Loves The One (That Loves The Lord)' was just another blues song, alerting listeners to their many failings in a manner that recalled the more doctrinal sermons favoured by the Catholic and Presbyterian churches. For someone who railed against the conventions of organised religion, Harrison was veering closer and closer to ministerial practices with every passing chord, cadence and lick: 'I wrote a song called 'Living In The Material World', and it was from that I decided to call the foundation the Material World Foundation. Most people would think of the material world as representing money and greed purely and take offence. But in my view, it means a physical world'.

The sharp and biting 'The Day The World Gets 'Round' – a scintillating number washed in Dylan's influence – featured Harrison's most rounded opinion on the shifting global landscapes that were occurring before him. Still reeling from what he perceived as selfishness from the tax departments, his anger culminates in one of the most detailed – and certainly one of the densest – recordings of his career. 'I look for the pure of heart/And the ones who have made a start', he cries, equally as unsure of his place in the pantheon of charity as the money men he'd been vilifying since 1966.

In style and content, 'The Day The World Gets 'Round' anticipated the folk revival of the late-1970s when such luminaries as John Martyn and Billy Bragg deviated from spectacle to more authentic textures. As it happens, Harrison had one immediate artistic peer in Cat Stevens: a fellow singer-songwriter determined to use his voice for spiritual and social change. Fittingly, Stevens (now known as Yusuf Islam) recorded a version of 'The Day The World Gets 'Round' in 2009. ' The song speaks of the split nature of this world', said the 'Peace Train' composer, 'comparing the love and joy of sharing what we all have on this earth, with the 'foolishness in man' and his quest for more, thus causing war and loss in the process'.

And then there's 'Be Here Now': a sparse ballad that may have been inspired by Jeff Buckley's startling 'Song To The Siren'. With little to shelter him but a piano and bass, Harrison's voice is presented with less flair than the more-lush vocal tracks presented elsewhere on the album. Somewhere between the piano swirl and the staccato bass comes the sound of a drone – no hollow metaphor, but a sitar returning from the attic to the world of Harrison. But like the guitars that open the track, the sitar has a functional role, resisting any temptation to perform a protracted solo that may temporarily distract listeners from the message. No tricks, no fades, just sheer unvarnished passion.

Voorman, for one, was captivated by the track's magic: 'I remember we were playing it, and I said, 'I'd love to play the upright bass on that', Voorman admitted in conversation with Simon Leng. 'And it was difficult to record, so I went into the bathroom at Friar Park, and the microphone was put in there. What happened was that Mal Evans came and flushed the toilet while I was playing the bass! I did a drawing of that, and it was still there at Friar Park in that bathroom the last time I was there'. Remembering his friend in 2021, Voorman dismissed the nickname that followed Harrison in death: 'He wasn't quiet at all', the painter/bass player pointed out.

An unkind listener might still be able to find fault with the album. Some of the tracks – such as the harrowing 'Don't Let Me Wait Too Long' and the choppy 'Sue Me, Sue You Blues' – feel like they're continuing the Shakespearian tragedy that began with the inconclusive *Let It Be* sessions. And, at times, *Living in the Material World* could benefit from a louder chorus, as was heard on the startling 'Try Some, Buy Some' and to a certain extent on the title track. Anyone hoping for the rock guitarist who'd composed 'Taxman' and 'Savoy Truffle', had bought the wrong album entirely.

But to the more open-minded, the album has tremendous depth –
especially in the lyrics: far-reaching and insightful in their delivery. 'The
Light That Has Lighted The World' married the awe and the anger that
typified Harrison's work, particularly in the opening verse:

So hateful of anyone that is happy or free
They live all their lives without looking to see
The light that has lighted the world

Harrison was 30, and although that scarcely qualified him as young, he
did prove remarkably adept at capturing the complications, contradictions
and fury that exists within the human spirit. And by presenting the album
in such an undressed manner, he was throwing himself out into the arena,
with nothing to save him from scrutiny or scorn. The material may have
been ponderous, but he supplied some visual gags on the cover. When
fans first bought the album in 1973, they found a joke that was written
to rib McCartney's earnest attempts to found the Wings fan club. Anyone
interested in finding out more information about the Jim Keltner Fan Club
could do so by sending a 'stamped undressed elephant' to a Los Angeles
postbox. Eager to drive the point home, Harrison attached a symbol
of a pair of wings, and only the most gullible would've missed out on
the pointed jab. But the joke was in keeping with the album's seditious
nature and only helped to highlight the division between those feasting
on their celebrity status and those who ached to hide from it. What it
does showcase is Harrison's desire to give people their due, no matter
what role they played in his music, and it was time Keltner got some
recognition for the myriad drum performances he'd laid down on tape.

Curiously, Eric Clapton's name did not feature in the credits. Having
recorded one stellar album as Derek and the Dominos, Clapton had
secluded himself from the world's prying eyes for the better part of
three years. In January 1973, Pete Townshend had managed to shake the
guitarist out of his exile for a concert later packaged as Eric Clapton's
Rainbow Concert. Faces guitarist Ronnie Wood joined the two musicians
to play slide, in a manner that differed greatly from Harrison's more
methodological style. The former Beatle didn't appear with the band, but
Clapton opened the set with 'Badge': a feisty pop number he'd completed
with Harrison in 1968. Clapton's musical career remained erratic, but he
had regained his footing and was in better spirits than he had been for
some time. His affection for Pattie Boyd remained as impassioned as ever,

and she was showing a greater interest in him. In 1974, Boyd followed her heart, and left Harrison for Clapton. 'It may have been two or three years before we became involved', Boyd summarised. 'Things were going so bad at home, my relationship with George was collapsing'. With all that in mind, it's not beyond the realms of imagination to assume that Harrison didn't want Clapton on *Living In The Material World*, but Clapton's pummelling performance style would've been inappropriate for an album that revels in ambience and atmosphere – the licks supporting the lyrics, as opposed to the more braggadocious style of guitar interplay heard on *All Things Must Pass*.

Above and beyond the trappings, Harrison single-handedly managed to create a new musical language that he wanted to share with the world. Like so many of his peers (Bob Dylan, Robbie Robertson, Billy Preston), he could only maintain an interest in his work if the work spoke to the vibrancy of the moment. By the album presenting to the world his many deep-rooted, undressed truths, it kept him from drowning in a career he had inadvertently started'. And like all his best work, it came from a place of tremendous commitment. *Living In The Material World* remains – just as it was in 1973 – a work of great beauty.

1974: All The World's A Stage: Well, America Is

If 1970 was a year of great fortune for Harrison, 1974 was his year of tremendous *mis*fortune. Indeed, if he had valued his place in rock aristocracy, he would likely have described the year as his *annus horribilis*. He started 1974 anxious to wash himself in the glory of India, and closed it burned-out, beaten down and afraid for his sanity. His best friend had walked off with his wife, his music wasn't selling as it once had, and he was no longer the critical darling the countercultural press had hailed him as in 1971. Worse than that, he had nearly lost his voice, and alcohol was taking precedence over meditation. And yet, he also managed to create some thunderous work (much of it riveting) – both onstage and off – and though the *Dark Horse* tour did not take off as he had hoped, it now serves as the blueprint for the world music genre that was popular in the 1980s.

In February, he returned once more to India, purportedly to attend a ceremony at Ravi Shankar´s house. In the midst of chanting Vedic hymns, Harrison rekindled his connection to India, and this helped the singer reconnect with the importance of the present above all else. There he experienced the mindfulness that furnished his newest material, although, by the time *Dark Horse* was released, the singer-songwriter was scarcely in any mood to process the wonders of the world. 1974 was a year in which he made many inflammatory comments, some deeply upsetting for the fans who read them. Nobody could accuse him of having hidden his views about nationalism, but his vision of a world free from passports must've raised a few eyebrows: 'As soon as we can all have Planet Earth passports, I'll be grateful, because I'm tired of being British or being white, or being a Christian or a Hindu', Harrison quipped. 'I don't have a philosophy; I just believe in the sap that runs throughout'.

Not everyone shared this viewpoint – as was evident in the UK – especially Northern Ireland, where the Republican movement was facing proud unionist opposition like Enoch Powell. In one sense, Harrison was carrying on the message that soaked Lennon's greatest anthem, 'Imagine', although, if Harrison was counting on Lennon's support, he was sorely mistaken. Having separated from Yoko Ono, Lennon had largely abandoned campaigning for any cause. But having put so much of his intellectual focus on being part of the trendy left, it took some time to recapture his lyrical voice. *Mind Games* – released in 1973 – was an insincere, even risible affair. McCartney tended not to make political proclamations if he could avoid it ('Give Ireland Back To The Irish' was a glorious exception to the rule he'd imposed on himself).

So this left Harrison alone in the 1970s as a spokesman for a countercultural cause, giving him some clout as he prepared for his third solo album. But unlike Lennon, Harrison saw no reason to compromise his music for the mass audience, and in doing so, robbed himself of the chance to release a track as indelible as 'Imagine'. He also threw caution to the wind with his surly behaviour, often responding to questions superciliously and with great reluctance. Asked why his output had slowed in recent times, Harrison replied, 'I've been busy working. I was busy being deposed (by Allen Klein). I've been doing some tracks of my own, did the Splinter album, finished up Ravi's album, been to India for two months, organised the music festival from India; I've done a million things'. Though snotty, this comment demonstrated his exhaustion, particularly after dedicating much of his productive and intellectual energy to the debut Splinter album *The Place I Love*.

Considering Harrison's métier, he likely relished the opportunity to plug in and wail (He was often too focused on his vocals to work out a guitar solo on his records), and invited stalwarts Klaus Voorman, Billy Preston and Jim Keltner to work on Splinter's debut with him. The first album released on the *Dark Horse* label, *The Place I Love,* demonstrates Harrison's innate musicality, and listening to it in 2021, it sounds like the prototype for his own studio masterpiece *Extra Texture (Read All About It)*. Free to join in with the musicians, Harrison was experimenting with a wider mosaic of instruments on the Splinter album, comfortable in the knowledge that he didn't have to worry about the vocals. The album finds the musician playing guitar, bass, synthesizer and harmonium, although his most notable contribution was the mandolin on 'Gravy Train'. There was no sitar, but Harrison did play dobro on 'Drink All Day (Got To Find Your Own Way Home)', and was even encouraged to sing along to 'Situation Vacant'. Creative as ever, he was perhaps exerting himself too much, and with a tour looming, Harrison might've been better off taking a less hands-on approach.

As 'Be Here Now' had demonstrated a year earlier, Harrison's interests lay in the present, regardless of any work sculpted in the preceding years. The efforts of the tour were the by-product of a songwriter working on the here and now – something he was eager to reiterate at a press conference in October 1974: 'It's definitely not going to be a Bangladesh mark II, if that's what people are thinking'. No doubt about it, Harrison was in no mood for compromise, but the Los Angeles conference at least offered listeners the chance to back out of the gig if they wanted to. It's also likely that Harrison misjudged the USA, and may have found it easier to market himself to a European audience, which was traditionally more open to esoteric genre hybrids. But true to his word, he agreed to perform there, even if it meant contending with a market more eager to welcome back a pop hero rather than the visionary that history is finally unveiling him as.

It was customary for 1960s artists to mythologise their careers with a tidy selection of favourites, fillers and obscure numbers, but Harrison seemed uninterested in giving audiences a helping they could easily get from their vinyl collection. Rather, he seemed happy to take a leaf out of Bob Dylan's book, and rearranged his back catalogue, regaling the audience with soulful-if-subversive renditions of the material that bore his writing credit. Unlike The Concert For Bangladesh, Harrison was unwilling to surrender his artistic impulses for the show, and the material – patchy though some of it was – was nevertheless an extension of his artistic trajectory, as well as his convictions.

Perhaps the most intriguing aspect of the American tour was that it coincided with the nation's renewed interest in The Beatles. Like Wings seminal *Band On The Run*, Lennon's *Walls and Bridges* made a more concentrated effort to tap into The Beatle blueprint and represented a triumphant cocktail of anger and melody. McCartney had seemingly abandoned rock for adult-oriented pop, but the blues-oriented 'Let Me Roll It' offered a guitar sound that would not have sounded out of place on the first three Beatle albums. Starr was enjoying chart success with a series of bouncy pop tunes, and America was happy to provide a market Britain had largely abandoned for a younger and more-trendy generation of musicians. The smart move was to pander to the Beatles fans, but Harrison simply wasn't interested in donning the mop-top or performing another rendition of 'If I Needed Someone'.

Sick of being mistaken for a former Beatle reclaiming his pop crown, Harrison made a conscious decision to rework some of the songs to reflect the new sound he was currently exploring. Glaringly, 'Something' was retooled almost entirely into something more plodding, culminating in a vocal performance that did little to dispel his ambivalence for the crowds or the gig. Worse than that, he altered the lines to John Lennon's 'In My Life' as a vehicle to express his devotion to God ('I love *him* more'). Audiences had long used rock as their form of rebellion against conservatism and religion, forming their new philosophies based on the records that helped spell out a new lexicon for them. Imagine what it must've been like for them coming face to face with a Beatle using his platform to wreck everything they held dear through a collection of elegies and spiritual hymns. And yet Harrison simply had to work this way. Rock music didn't have the same hold over him as it did in the 1950s, but Shankar's work – dexterous, ambitious and stemming from a place of great ritualism and practice – more than compensated for that empty void.

Harrison's work had won him an unprecedented level of critical acclaim in the early-1970s, but gradually this level of appreciation had begun to wind down. Having elected to record his third album, Harrison confounded further expectations by agreeing to undertake an American tour, making him the first solo Beatle to do so. Extreme as he'd ever been, he recognised the importance of the tour. He purportedly said in the days before the Vancouver show: 'I either finish this tour ecstatically happy and want to go on tour everywhere, or I'll end up just going back to my cave for another five years'.

Mindful of his experiences in The Beatles, Harrison opted to give the musicians as few instructions as possible. In *While My Guitar Gently Weeps: The Music of George Harrison*, Andy Newmark portrayed Harrison as a corporal, joining his men on the battlefield: '...he hated being a leader and wasn't comfortable being the leader – he hated giving orders, he wasn't at all a pushy superstar or egotistical. He was totally the opposite of all that'.

Harrison's experience of touring differed vastly from the spectacles 1970s audiences now demanded, and unlike the more amenable McCartney, he wasn't particularly interested in pandering to the crowd. He recalled in 1979: 'With the Beatles, we used to do 30 minutes on stage, and we could get it down to 25 minutes if we did it fast. We were on and off and 'thank you' and back to the hotel. Suddenly to have to be playing two and one-half hours for 47 gigs, flying all 'round, I was wasted'. At a press conference, Harrison was once again queried about whether The Beatles would reform: 'I don't think The Beatles were that good', he said. 'I think they're fine, you know'. McCartney? 'Paul is a fine bass player, but he's a bit overpowering at times...'. He didn't stop there: 'To tell the truth, I'd join a band with John Lennon any day. But I couldn't join a band with Paul McCartney. It's nothing personal, it's just from a musical point of view'. Harrison was not in a healthy place, but optimistic as ever, he was happy to put his life in the hands of a higher power: 'I only met

Andy Newmark and Willie Weeks a few months ago. If I hadn't met them, I wouldn't have a rhythm section, but I believe the Lord provides me or you or all of us. If you believe that, he provides you with whatever you need'.

Dark Horse

Personnel:

George Harrison: vocals, electric guitar, acoustic guitar, Moog synthesizer, clavinet, organ, bass, gubguba, drums, percussion

Alvin Lee: electric guitar

Robben Ford: electric and acoustic guitar

Mick Jones: acoustic guitar

Billy Preston: piano, electric piano, organ

Nicky Hopkins, Gary Wright: piano

Roger Kellaway: piano, organ

Tom Scott: saxophone, flute, organ

Jim Horn, Chuck Findley: flute

Willie Weeks, Klaus Voormann, Max Bennett: bass

Ringo Starr, Jim Keltner, John Guerin: drums

Andy Newmark: drums, percussion

Emil Richards: percussion, wobble board

Lon Van Eaton, Derrek Van Eaton: backing vocals

Record Label: Apple

Recorded November 1973, April 1974, August–October 1974, at FPSHOT, Oxfordshire; A&M, Los Angeles Produced by George Harrison

Release dates: UK: 20 December 1974, US: 30 May 1973

Chart placings: UK: Did not chart, US: 4

Running Time: 41:19

If he lacked Lennon's raw thunder or McCartney's attention to stagecraft, Harrison's band compensated with musicality that could shift his Beatle material from mere covers into cerebral, subversive works of art. Better still, Harrison emerged from the rafters, buoyed by coiled emotional intensity and a desire to champion change. He was – he told an audience in Vancouver – prepared to die for Indian music, but not for rock and roll, and he highlighted the importance of change in the aforementioned press conference. The Beatles were yesterday's music; Harrison expected everyone, including himself, to live in the present.

On 2 November 1974, he performed the first show of the American tour. In striking contrast to the more-ornate displays typically favoured by glam artists like David Bowie and Marc Bolan, the tour was a more sedate affair, and any moments of tension or drama were to be deduced through the instrumental passages, and not through a tidy flourish from the performer in question. The calibre of musicianship was high, particularly among the musicians chosen by Ravi Shankar. Seated with Shankar, were Alla Rakha, Shivkumar Sharma, Lakshmi Shankar, Hariprasad Chaurasia, L. Subramaniam and Sultan Khan: precocious musicians who were largely unheard of on the western circuit. Their music was among the most personal and emotionally-vibrant work that sat in Harrison's record collection. But if the job was to exposure then to greater popularity, it wasn't entirely successful. 'George says people expect him to be exactly what he was ten years ago', Shankar said. 'He's matured so much in so many ways. That's the problem with all the artists, I suppose'. Harrison countered, 'I realise The Beatles did fill a space in the sixties', but he felt that enough time had elapsed since then: 'People are afraid of change'.

An interesting addition to the Dark Horse tour was the band's bluesy makeover of 'While My Guitar Gently Weeps' – Harrison's moribund vocal delivery offering a more hypnotic quality to a lyric steeped in brooding introversion. There was a sense that his demons were spiralling out of control, and his tone was getting worse.

Fans who bought tickets to the gigs were met with a series of proclamations: some of them laughable, but most of them confrontational. Worse still, Harrison had developed a habit of criticising audience members during concerts. It was hardly Roger Waters spitting at the audiences who had made him rich, but Harrison's sourness felt out of place in a country that had held onto The Beatles flame long after British audiences had ditched the Liverpool favourites for newer, shinier fads.

As an added twist, the tour featured the two ensembles performing as one voice, offering audiences the chance to hear the endless possibilities that musicians of three continents could contribute. Fittingly, Harrison was distancing himself from his English heritage and was advocating the importance of shared communities. In one sense, the tour presented an absolute realisation of a dream Harrison had been building towards, uniting audiences to witness the birth of the next stage in music. But the harder he tried to invite listeners, the vaster the gap grew, and he found himself bellowing at audiences, as opposed to luring them into the musical pool he'd designed for them. He might've held onto the beard, but this was not the guru of 1971, and his influence was certainly dwindling. One night, he couldn't hold it in any longer and shouted, 'I'm

Right: 1974 was a difficult year for Harrison, but there were some happy moments, such as visiting Gerald Ford's White House.

Left: 'Twooo love.' George and Olivia were together until his death in 2001.

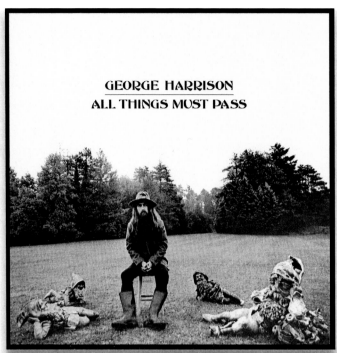

Above: The former Beatle sits in a circle of gnomes for the cover of *All Things Must Pass*. Is he having a laugh or making a point? (*Apple*)

Above: The Beatles were history, and Harrison was eager to discover new avenues for himself.

Right: 'What is Life?' is a stunning effort, showing his maturity as a songwriter, and his confidence as an arranger. *(Apple)*

GEORGE HARRISON
what is life / apple scruffs

APPLE 1828

Above: Harrison's first and finest work, *All Things Must Pass*, was reissued in a stunning special edition in 2021 to mark its 50th anniversary. *(Beatles Solo)*

Above: George Harrison is caught playing lead guitar for a John Lennon album. His work was as riveting as Lennon's lyrics were hackneyed.

Right: Harrison saw his instrument as the next logical step of his meditative journey. Here he's playing lead guitar on Lennon's 'How Do You Sleep?'

Above: Harrison appeared on *The Dick Cavett Show* during the 1970s.

Below: He may have smiled on *The Dick Cavett Show,* but things weren't so rosy behind the scenes at this time.

Left: *Concert for Bangladesh.* Anxious to highlight the importance of the event, Harrison utilised a series of harrowing photos to rally support around the project. (*Apple*)

Right: Brandishing a beard during the concert, Harrison was distancing himself from the more regimented look of the early Beatles.

Left: Paul McCartney and John Lennon declined their invitations, but Ringo Starr duly turned up to The Concert for Bangladesh.

Right: The Concert for Bangladesh paved the way for large-scale charity concerts like Live Aid and Live 8.

Left: Yes, that's Eric Clapton on guitar on the far right. He was one of Harrison's best pals.

Right: The concert was a triumph, both as a form of altruism and a musical exhibition of talent.

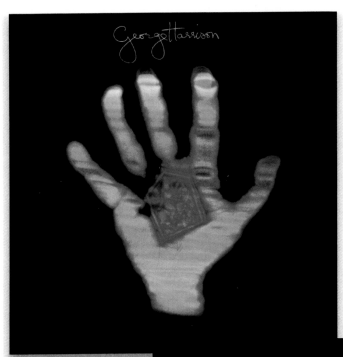

Left: *Living in the Material World*. It wasn't a sequel to *All Things Must Pass*, but this record still held tremendous power and beauty.

Right: Harrison was determined to bring light and shade into his art, and 'Give Me Love (Give Me Peace On Earth)' was a formidable hybrid.

Right: Arguably the most overlooked album in Harrison's canon, *Dark Horse* continues to divide people to this day. (*Apple*)

Left: *Dark Horse* represents everything that was far-reaching, vulnerable and exhilarating about Harrison. This is its back cover. (*Apple*)

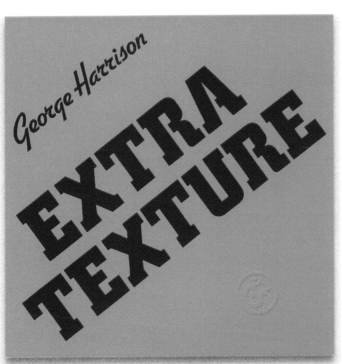

Left: Where *Dark Horse* was uncompromising and jagged, *Extra Texture* was jaunty and recorded with tremendous attention to detail. (*Apple*)

Right: Representing something of a creative rebirth for Harrison, he produced one of his best albums in 1975. This is the back cover. (*Apple*)

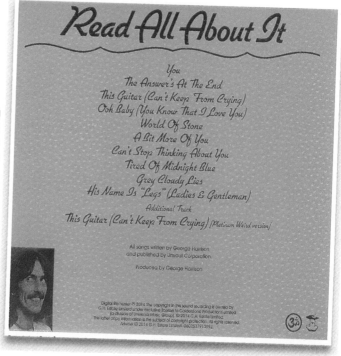

Read All About It

You
The Answer's At The End
This Guitar (Can't Keep From Crying)
Ooh Baby (You Know That I Love You)
World Of Stone
A Bit More Of You
Can't Stop Thinking About You
Tired Of Midnight Blue
Grey Cloudy Lies
His Name Is "Legs" (Ladies & Gentleman)

Additional Track
This Guitar (Can't Keep From Crying) (Platinum Weird version)

All songs written by George Harrison
and published by Umlaut Corporation.

Produced by George Harrison

Right: Harrison was in a tricky situation: he was getting sued over copyright issues with 'My Sweet Lord'. The contemporary album *Thirty Three and 1/3* did little to showcase his brilliance. (*Dark Horse*)

SIDE I
Woman Don't You Cry For Me
Dear One
Beautiful Girl
This Song
See Yourself

SIDE II
It's What You Value
True Love
Pure Smokey
Crackerbox Palace
Learning How To Love You

Left: But the album does boast 'This Song', which discussed the legal situation he found himself in.

Left: Ricky Fataar as Stig O'Hara, the George of The Rutles.

Right: The Rutles were bigger than Rod, you know! *The Rutles: All You Need Is Cash* was as cutting as it was reverent; a brilliant film.

Below: Ron, Dirk, Stig and Barry: The Rutles.

Right: Director Richard Lester felt Harrison was a natural actor, as is evident from this clip.

Left: Monty Python alum Michael Palin enjoyed a real-life friendship with Harrison.

Right: Everyone wants to dress up as a Beatle. Eric Idle just went one further!

George Harrison

Left: And then the Beatle re-emerged from the creative wilderness as a father. This newfound joy seeped into his work with the eponymous *George Harrison*.

Right: The erstwhile Beatle had a new hairstyle; curly. He was free to and anxious to marry.

Right: Notoriously private, Harrison was beginning to embrace the video format by the end of the 1970s.

Left: The promo for 'Blow Away' was one of the most enjoyable of his career.

Right: The new album was a strong return to form and generated strong notices from the media.

Above: Handmade Films helped revive the British Film Industry and produced a number of interesting films, particularly in the 1980s.

Right: George Harrison bankrolled *Life of Brian*. God bless him for it!

Below: *The Long Good Friday* was an incendiary film and exhibits a career-best performance from Bob Hoskins.

not up here jumping like a loony for my own sake, but to tell you that the Lord is in your hearts. Somebody's got to tell you'. To no one's surprise, Harrison opted not to commemorate this event with another live LP.

The *Dark Horse* album offers an interesting bridge between the more pastoral *Living In The Material World* and the giddily inventive *Extra Texture(Read All About It)*, retaining some of the former's solemn atmosphere but lacking some of the lush detail that made up the latter; *Dark Horse* setting sparky guitar licks over a sprightly rhythm section Harrison intended for the live stage. The protracted instrumental passages stand as a crossroads between the two better-celebrated albums, but *Dark Horse* was ultimately written as a live document, offering listeners a map for the upcoming American shows.

Kicking off *Dark Horse* was 'Hari's On Tour': a choppy instrumental, rife with energy, enthusiasm and cracked humour. He was growing more confident as a slide player, which was ideal for a man losing some of the nuance from his voice, and some of the tracks are given new leases of life when the slide appears. In many ways, the slide stood as his true voice, decorating the soundscape with the tears he ached to let out ('So Sad') and imitating the bursts of thunder anxious to leave the composer's ever-excitable mind ('Maya Love').

Whatever the album's flaws (and there are many), it duly exhibited some of the most accomplished, and indelible guitar hooks of his post-Beatle career. Moreover, Harrison had elected to not just record an instrumental but to concede many of the guitar duties to Robben Ford. Harrison had caught wind of Tom Scott at a Joni Mitchell concert in London and invited the saxophonist to perform many of the more intricate solos heard on the record. Perhaps best-known as the man behind the *Starsky & Hutch* theme, Scott was a saxophone player of some repute and had worked with seminal jazz organist Richard 'Groove' Holmes on some of his recordings. From Jimmy Webb to Tom Waits, Scott had worked with artists of every persuasion, but in his heart he was a team player and excelled in a band format. Fusion album *Tom Scott and The L.A. Express* demonstrated his credentials, the horns flitting in and out of the work. In later years, he would play the saxophone for Rod Stewart's pounding 'Da Ya Think I'm Sexy' (not forgetting Scott's fiery solo on the Wings classic 'Listen To What The Man Said'), but Harrison recognised in Scott a like-minded spirit who could thrive as both a front-person and a sideman.

Unlike the more leisurely *Living In The Material World*, many of the tracks that ended up on *Dark Horse* were recorded quickly and with terrific style. His was a stripped-back form of rock that had parellels with the punk posturings of late seventies rock, rather than the proto-prog approach the Beatles albums *Sgt. Pepper's Lonely Hearts Club Band* and *The White Album* had taken. Weirdly, the cover owed more to The Beatles than the material might've suggested: *Dark Horse*, like *Sgt. Pepper* before it opens up like a collage of luminaries, each garnering a spot in the picture. A joke on Harrison's part? If the album had a flippancy, it was buried deep beneath the tremolo guitar licks and moments of stark-naked introspection, and it's no hyperbole that *Dark Horse* is ultimately remembered as his darkest offering.

Harrison had no issues abandoning his Beatle image, but in doing so, he was seen in some quarters as overly zealous and opportunistic. The video for 'Ding Dong, Ding Dong' offered him the chance to poke fun at this misconception, and he duly appeared in his *Sgt. Pepper* outfit for the promo film. Although he'd worn a moustache for the 1967 album cover, he now looked visibly older than the more baby-faced musician who had stood beside the performers that had paved the way for what rock and roll had become by the seventies. But the passion for music remained intact in 1974, and with 'Ding Dong, Ding Dong', he was offering a valedictorian anthem that his fans could cherish. But there's a critical difference between 'Ding Dong, Ding Dong' and the other elegies that Harrison was writing at that time in his life. The powerful 'Isn't It A Pity' and 'The Day The World Gets 'Round' were the work of a man eager to witness change in the world; 'Ding Dong, Ding Dong' finds the same person cherishing the gifts it has given him. And rather than write a Christmas single (already a hackneyed practice even by 1974), Harrison used this as an opportunity to compose a song for New Year's Eve: 'I was just sitting by the fire, playing the guitar, and I looked up on the wall, and there it was, carved into the wall in oak', Harrison recalled, happy as ever that his house of choice was feeding his muse.

If 'Ding Dong, Ding Dong' harked back to an earlier era, 'Far East Man' signalled a new genre of music entirely. Written with Ronnie Wood, the jagged guitar licks, shifting chords and air of cogitation, earmarked it as a genre which would be refurbished in the 1980s as world music. Wood had already recorded a shorter version on his biting *I've Got My Own Album To Do,* but Harrison's version was a richer experience, culminating in an instrumental coda echoing the wars he and his musical peers, a la Dylan, were so determined to end. Harrison was born during a war, he'd campaigned against wars, and with The Concert For Bangladesh, he'd worked to earn money for those ravaged by war. But behind this track stood a man weakened by his own personal battles and insecurities. The title 'Dark Horse', if little else, was an obvious dig at his standing in the eyes of the world. His critical notices were stronger than McCartney's; his singles were outselling Lennon's, but Harrison remained, as ever, a stranger in the world of pop. As he himself would say, 'The one nobody's bothered to put any money on. That's me I guess'.

Behind the obvious metaphor stood a more-steamy one: growing up in Liverpool, Harrison understood a dark horse to be someone who could fulfil a person's deep-rooted sexual desires. His list of conquests was many (Pattie Boyd herself suggested that something 'happened' between Harrison and Maureen Starkey: Ringo's wife), and much like Leonard Cohen, he felt there was a direct correlation between the sexual and the spiritual. Not everyone shared this opinion so liberally, and there were likely murmurings that Harrison was using his doctrines to disguise his sexual fantasies. '(George) liked the things that men like', chuckled McCartney in the 2011 Martin Scorsese documentary. 'He was red-blooded'. 'Dark Horse' sets out to explain Harrison's point of view. He had little interest in discussing any transgressions with any hotheaded journalist swooping for a headline. Everyone had their own secrets to hide, so why was he expected to oblige their requests? The message of the song seems to be 'admit to your failings, and I'll spill mine', although his anger – largely contained for the majority of the song – eventually spirals out in the song's final verse:

I thought that you knew it all along
Until you started getting me not right
Seems as if you heard a little late
I warned you when we both was at the starting gate

Even as late as 1974, Harrison was being underestimated by both his peers and the press, but if he was anxious to get an apology, then he should've waited for his voice to heal. The vocal on 'Dark Horse' sounds ragged, and it sounded even worse on stage as Harrison – chiefly a backing singer – tried to replicate the complicated performance of the recording. There was no doubt about it: he'd taken on too much, and judging by the tapes we have from the concerts, keyboardist Billy Preston ultimately sounds much sharper. However, after more than 40 shows that explored blues, soul, funk, slide and smatterings of eastern-oriented rock, the fatigue had taken hold of the singer. Irritated by the constraints of rock-and-roll stage patter, the guitarist would not go on another tour until 1991. By that time, Harrison had re-emerged as a more-relaxed musician and performed 'Something' as if honouring the backing of the original record.

The Harrison of 1974 had little interest in pandering to the rigours of rock and roll, which might explain why his material felt so distantly removed from the pop work of his best-known group. But even if the audiences weren't drawn to the tour, Harrison was enjoying the work his bandmates were laying down. He felt that Willie Weeks was a formidable bass player, and behind them lay the footwork of Jim Keltner: a percussionist Ringo Starr happily referred to as his peer. Then there was the presence of Ravi Shankar: the musician who had opened Harrison's eyes in the late-1960s. Like Dylan, Shankar recognised the artist within the guitar player, and buoyed by the encouragement, Harrison welcomed the sitarist onto the tour.

He took it upon himself to alter some of the lyrics to The Beatles' standards on the Dark Horse tour. It was a brave move, but in the eyes of an audience eager to watch a Beatle, his alterations were ill-advised.He changed some of the lyrics of 'In My Life' to reflect his standing as a man of faith, and altered 'Something''s more-carefree tone to express a certain contempt for the institution of marriage – 'Find yourself another lover', he growled, croaking behind a burning guitar lick and thunderous organ licks. It might've sounded ugly, but coming from the mouth of someone undergoing divorce, it typified a man who was happier to shout out his feelings than disguise them.

Yet accusations of haughtiness were wide of the mark. The concerts were undeniably mainstream, keeping themselves to a solid length that was expected of a rock concert. And in one sense, Harrison was keeping the spirit of The Beatles alive by steadfastly refusing to acquiesce to expectations. It was a brave – if slightly naive – action on his part, yet the tour should be remembered as a noble failure rather than the grand folly so many pencil it as.

To his credit, Harrison had forged a solid reputation based on principle, precision and emotional honesty, so the lyrics – read apart from the influence of the ragged, wrenching guitar patterns – still fit within the world he'd built as a solo artist. There was the coiled intensity of 'Far East Man', the spiritual longing of 'It Is He (Jai Sri Krishna)', and the emotion that poured out of 'Simply Shady'. Stability was restored with the one-two punch of 'Bye Bye Love' and 'Ding Dong, Ding Dong', the former a sprighly uptempo pop song written in the 1950s, the latter a pounding chorus-heavy single determined for a commercial audience. In some ways, the album was more tuneful than its immediate word-heavy predecessor, but the ragged edges, croaky vocal performances and lengthy instrumental passages (not forgetting the fact it wasn't released before the American tour) made it hard for more-conservative audiences to swallow. Some of the band were underwhelmed by the material presented to them. 'I didn't have the sense at the time that I was part of anything biblical', Andy Newmark says in Graeme Thomson's *George Harrison: Behind The Locked Door*. 'I knew he was coming off big records with *All Things Must Pass* and *Living In The Material World*, and I don't think *Dark Horse* came anywhere near that. It didn't reach those heights. They were nice tunes, he was a good songwriter, he had a great style as a player, but I didn't think that record was going to bring down the heavens'. While the album didn't make Harrison rich (to this day, it's still one of his least-popular works), it made him human, and the failings that turned off 1970s listeners are the very aspects that make it so compelling all these decades later.

Cocaine was becoming a prominent fixture in Harrison's life. To some, his predilection for powder seemed at odds with the message he was supposedly trying to spread. But according to Pete Townshend – another rock artist searching to use his platform to spread the word of love – the two habits were not necessarily unaligned: 'I think a lot of us thought we already knew. I remember having a conversation with George Harrison about how he could reconcile following Krishna with his having to lay out lines of coke in order to talk about Krishna with me'. Whether it was prayer or powder that led to nirvana, there was no doubt that Harrison was experiencing personal turmoil. 'George used coke excessively, and I think it changed him', Patti Boyd wrote in *Wonderful Tonight*. 'Cocaine was different, and I think it froze George's emotions and hardened his heart'. Harrison's throwaway cover of 'Bye Bye Love', carried with it a thinly-veiled barb at his wife's choice of lover:

There goes our lady, with a-you-know-who
I hope she's happy, old Clapper too
We had good rhythm (and a little slide) till she stepped in
Did me a favour
I... threw them both out

Although known for his cries of anguish, Harrison had tempered any ill-feeling for his wife, in favour of a jocular rocker, and any anger the songwriter held for the man now sleeping with her was quickly disguised in a bawdy pun. And however misanthropic he appeared to the critics, it's to his credit that whenever a journalist gathered the courage to question him about his love life, he categorically refused to enter into discourse about Boyd. Even more remarkably, Harrison refrained from making any incendiary comments about Clapton, even though there was ample opportunity to do so. Clapton's comments in 1976 don't bear repeating, but they were definitely at odds with the open-minded politics of Harrison's oeuvre. Rather, Harrison opted to admire Clapton's guitar prowess, particularly the way he could come up with fizzling solos on the spot.

In 1974, comedy armoured Harrison at press conferences, as it had in the 1960s: 'I'd rather she be with him than some dope'. Lest we forget that Harrison was no cherub either: the reported list of his extramarital affairs is long, and he was no stranger to sleeping with a pal's wife. In 2007, Boyd confirmed that Harrison had a liaison with Maureen Starkey: a move that caused Boyd great sorrow. No doubt it hurt Ringo too!

Dark Horse is an album of pain, pathos and purging violence; Harrison's guitar ricocheting through the cylinders without shame, grimly committed to exposing the artist's pain through a collection of pummelling licks, each more ferocious than the last. In some ways, this was his *Plastic Ono Band*, his *Blood On The Tracks*, his great expression of agony in a decade that showed little of the 1960s idealism. *Dark Horse* has one glaring drawback: the vocal performances – ragged and damaged by a throat infection – sound tired, and tortured by the demands of the music. When the material warranted a more-damning performance ('Simply Shady'), the harder-edged tones added to the drama. But on the softer tracks, Harrison sounded cragged, leading many listeners to query the reason to record the album under duress. No sooner had he completed the album, than a cruel joke circulated among the press: that the album was more 'Dark Hoarse' than *Dark Horse*.

Never the greatest singer in the world, Harrison nonetheless could lend his voice to most genres, but his punctured, flat vocal deliveries on *Dark Horse* were a godsend for trendy journalists determined to knock The Beatles off their pedestal – and boy did they go for him! *Rolling Stone* called it a 'disastrous album'; the *NME* thought it 'stuff and nonsense', and *The Village Voice* considered Harrison a 'hoarse dork'. Writing for *High Fidelity*, Mike Jahn delivered the hardest blow, suggesting that the

US Food and Drug Administration arrest Harrison for 'selling a sleeping pill without a prescription'. Lennon likely would've waved the criticisms off as 'It's only a bloody record', but Harrison had a tour to promote and couldn't afford to be so insouciant facing the press. Looking back on the reviews, they read like the childish tantrums of a group of men disappointed that their hero had failed to measure up to the standard they expected of him, and rather than embrace the album on its own merits, they chose to deride the artist instead of his art. If Harrison was deflated by the audience's apathy towards his spiritual dissertation, it was nothing compared to the effect the negative reviews had on him. His voice was shattered, his confidence fading, and he was spending much of his free time recuperating from the gigs. In one of the more revealing moments in Martin Scorsese's documentary, we see Harrison gargling over a sink, in a last-minute attempt to revive his vocal cords. He needed to chant and sing:

Maya love, Maya love
The love is like the rain
Beating on your window brain

Maya love, Oh Maya love,
My love is like a stream
Flowing through this cosmic dream

But Harrison still had fans in the US, one of them the son of the President. Jack Ford attended a concert in Salt Lake City, Utah, before extending an invitation to the band to visit the White House. The first ex-Beatle granted a meeting with a President, Harrison was impressed with the way Gerald Ford conducted himself: 'He seemed very relaxed. He was much easier to meet than I would expect'. Unlike his son, Gerald Ford wasn't too familiar with Harrison's work, but the musician didn't seem too bothered by this. What photos there are of the event show a man clearly enjoying himself. As a boy who'd grown up on American cinema and music, Harrison had long felt a connection to the country, so it must've been a delight to be asked into the office of its leader. And at a time when there was very little to comfort Harrison, he could at least walk away from 1974 with one positive memory to look back on.

Though Harrison had recorded gritty-sounding guitar passages for other artists -'Sour Milk Sea' (Jackie Lomax), 'Gimme Some Truth'(John Lennon), 'Back Off Boogaloo' (Ringo Starr) – he rarely let his guitar wail away on his own records. 'Simply Shady' is an exception to the rule, and the licks – blistering behind a mosaic of broken promises from a time of unfulfillment – cement the anger, soaking listeners in the rage that was bubbling out of his mouth and into the microphone. Harrison wrote in *I Me Mine*: 'There was a bad domestic year, 1974. All that splitting up around the house. 'Simply Shady', that song is about it. At the same time, I was doing a Splinter album and a Ravi Shankar album and my own album, and then during rehearsals, I was trying to finish my album, and in the end, Denis O'Brien carried me out of the studio to my first concert (in Canada) because I was trying to finish the album in time to get it out to coincide with the tour, which is the way the *business* needs it'.

The hauntingly beautiful 'So Sad' is also one of the few songs to feature a hummable chorus: clouding the sadness with a melody that was pleasantly Dylanesque. Unlike on the album's more-intricate numbers, Harrison's lugubrious voice felt apposite for a song about changing seasons and fading memories. He recalled, 'It is so sad. It was at the time I was splitting up with Pattie'. The lyric – written in the third person – felt like a confession from the writer to his listeners as he wandered into a divorce even more personal than The Beatles breakup. Boyd was hurt too. But – publicly at least – she opted to remember the happy memories over the more painful ones. She told *The Times*: 'Even after we split, he was always my friend. We'd still speak on the phone'.

In many ways, the *Dark Horse* tour pinpointed the way to the world music genre's popularity in the eighties, but like many aspects of Harrison's career, it went largely unrecognised, while his artistic peers (including Paul Simon) would enjoy the credit for a genre the music-buying public had once thought inconceivable. The tour, while imperfect, set the stage for a new form of music, but Harrison was deeply bemused by the frosty response to a stagecraft he put his heart and soul into: 'It's a pity that a lot of people missed out on something that went above their heads', he sighed in 1977, but the damage was done. He wouldn't set out on tour again until the 1990s.

Ultimately, it did prove to the erstwhile Beatle that he couldn't leave his past behind, no matter how greatly he wished to part from it. However hard he fought to leave The Beatles behind, The Beatles would never leave *him* behind, and he found himself defined by a fame that no longer interested him. What that famous past did offer him was money, and the time had finally come for the band to collect the cash that had long evaded them.

Unlike the other Beatles, Lennon had spent much of the 1970s in creative withdrawal, and neither *Some Time In New York City* nor *Mind Games* (both recorded after having moved to America) showed any of the spark that had funnelled through The Beatles' exhilarating work. He had also separated from Yoko Ono, and now found himself in the arms of May Pang: a precocious woman in her 20s who featured on '#9 Dream': a triumphant return-to-form for the writer. Finally, he'd produced a work worthy of his name, and indeed *Walls and Bridges* was a superlative effort. It proved to be Lennon's most inventive work since 1970, and buoyed by his most recent creative endeavours (not least the number-1 US single 'Whatever Gets You Thru The Night' featuring Elton John on harmony vocals), he seemed more eager to work with McCartney and Harrison again. A ramshackle jam with McCartney was later bootlegged under the title *A Toot And A Snore In '74*, and Lennon also hinted to Harrison that he would appear at one of his concerts, much in the way he had made a cameo appearance at an Elton John gig.

Meanwhile, McCartney was in the throes of an incredible second wind of creativity, having penned one astonishingly-beautiful ballad ('My Love'), composed a stellar theme for Roger Moore's first James Bond movie *Live And Let Die*, and unveiled *Band On The Run* to the public: a progressive pop record that happily sat beside his best work with The Beatles. He and Linda had sat in one of Harrison's shows (in weird disguises), happy that many of the unpleasant court cases were behind them. McCartney and Harrison decided to meet up with Lennon in New York to dissolve the Beatles partnership in each other's presence. It meant collecting royalties that had been accruing since 1971, and – without a hit – Harrison appreciated the prospect of income. In a move that mirrored the final recording sessions, Harrison and McCartney turned up to complete the transaction, but Lennon was nowhere to be seen. McCartney remembered: 'He wouldn't come from across the park. George got on the phone and yelled, 'Take those fucking shades off and come over here, you''. Adding salt to the wound, Lennon sent over a balloon with a sign: 'Listen to this balloon'. Even for someone as cosmic as Harrison, this felt like a kick in the jaw. In May Pang's memoir *Loving John*, a terrifying confrontation emerges, and Harrison comes across as a man short on manners and burning on fury. It must've been devastating for Pang to sit through, but Harrison had lived in his own personal hell too long to care. It can't have been thrilling for Harrison to sit down with McCartney so soon after knocking his bass work, yet the two men were humble enough to put their differences aside for the sake of their shared history. Together, McCartney and Harrison exemplified maturity, reverence and respect: traits Lennon showed himself to be sorely lacking by virtue of his absence.

Instead, Lennon opted to sign the papers the following week during a trip to Disney World. Reconnecting with his son Julian, Lennon took a moment to jot his name on the papers that severed his ties to the 1960s. Who knows what went on in John Lennon's head as he signed his name, but whatever it was, it stayed with him. Yet, he must've been amused by the amusement rides, silhouettes and cartoon characters that awaited him beyond the rim of the funny papers in his hands. On 29 December 1974, Lennon dissolved the greatest band that had ever been, and joined his family at Disney World.

1975: The Dark Horse Rises

Extra Texture (Read All About It)
Personnel:
George Harrison: vocals, electric and acoustic guitar, piano, ARP and Moog synthesizers
David Foster: piano, tack piano, electric piano, organ, ARP synthesizer
Nicky Hopkins, Leon Russell: piano
Gary Wright: organ, electric piano, ARP synthesizer
Billy Preston: electric piano
Jesse Ed Davis: electric guitar
Klaus Voormann, Willie Weeks: bass
Paul Stallworth: bass, vocals
Jim Horn, Tom Scott: saxophone
Chuck Findley: trumpet, trombone
Jim Keltner, Jim Gordon: drums, percussion
Andy Newmark: drums
Ronnie Spector, 'Legs' Larry Smith: vocals
Norm Kinney: percussion
Record label: Apple
Recorded in November 1973, April 1974, August-October 1974, at FPSHOT, Oxfordshire; A&M, Los Angeles Produced by George Harrison
Release dates: UK: 3 October 1975, US: 22 September 1975
Chart placings: UK: 16, US: 8
Running Time: 41:19

Whatever failings the first Wings lineup endured were long ironed out with the presence of Jimmy McCulloch: a hotshot guitarist from Glasgow. His youth, vibrancy and guitar wizardry served McCartney well, and the 1975 album *Venus and Mars* (Wings' most rewarding to date) was awash with shimmering choruses, sophisticated orchestral arrangements and shrewd, soulful lyrics. Finding a drummer proved to be harder (Two percussionists performed on the record), but the band seemed fixed on Joe English by the time they embarked on their 1976 tour. McCartney – always the Beatle who relished the opportunity to sing live – had furnished a setlist so comfortable in its skin that the five included Beatles numbers seemed like the afterthought of a musician eager to embrace new challenges. With Denny Laine and Linda by his side, McCartney sounded more confident than he had in the 1960s, and the songs that had been met with scorn in the wake of the Beatles breakup were now being rewarded by members of the curmudgeonly British press. 'They say 'Sgt Pepper' was the best period for me,' McCartney told *Melody Maker*, 'and it was the best music at the time, but some of the stuff that happens now is better than The Beatles.'

While McCartney embraced his well-earned celebrity, Harrison couldn't have shown less interest in that particular element of show business: 'You know, I don't see my music anymore as being top-20 somehow', the guitarist admitted to WNEW-FM. 'It matters more to me that I can simply sing it better, play it better and, with less orchestration, get over more feeling'.

1974 was a difficult year for Harrison. Lost in a sea of drugs, drink and divorce, he was beginning to feel disconnected from the world. For the first time in his solo career, he found himself at an impasse, so he began sheltering himself in the comfort of his garden and home. Returning to his domestic sanctuary, his worst moments awaited him as he wandered from the plane to the garden plains of Friar Park. He recalled: 'When I got off the plane and back home, I went into the garden and I was so relieved. That was the nearest I got to a nervous breakdown. I couldn't even go into the house'.

Fortunately, his financial credit was healthy, and he was now free to enjoy the earnings stockpiled from The Beatles' trusts. And in Olivia Arias, he had found friendship, dependability, and most importantly, love. They met through Dark Horse Records, where Arias worked as a receptionist. Coinciding with the difficult American tour, Harrison could find some solace in that it introduced him to the woman he would spend the rest of his life with. He was smitten, and his close friends were quick to recognise the effect. Drummer Jim Keltner remembered: 'Olivia came into the picture at just the right time; a crazy, dark time. She is a strong person, and when he fell for her, we all agreed that was a good thing. It wasn't good for him to be on his own, and without her, things would have got worse'. The feeling was clearly mutual, and when Arias was asked if it was love at first sight, she replied, 'Pretty much. We felt it in our hearts from before we met. Even on the phone, we seemed to have some understanding, like you do when you meet the right person'.

Many artists, once they reach a certain level of success, find it more appealing to set up their own label than to continue with the regulations set by an established company. For less-mainstream artists, the process and production are more rewarding than the audience's validation of the work. And with Apple Records winding down, Harrison was in the perfect place to start his own label. The prospect of buying Apple and running it with Ringo Starr was tempting, but ultimately Harrison opted to explore an entirely different path. He learned a great deal from his time at Apple and still felt it was a model to follow: 'It went crazy in the end, Apple', Harrison admitted in 1975, 'but it did give some good people an outlet. That's why I'm here now with Dark Horse Records – Apple didn't shake my faith that much. Good musicians are worth encouraging'.

Ravi Shankar was an early find, as was Henry McCullough, curiously enough. The Portstewart-born guitar player had left Wings in 1973 and released his pointedly titled *Mind Your Own Business* in the years after. Considering Harrison's past experiences with Paul McCartney, the irony can't have escaped McCullough that he was joining a label owned by a Beatle. But whatever the circumstances, *Mind Your Own Business* was a stellar recording, replete with vigour, romance and dazzling guitar effects.

But rich pickings for *Dark Horse* could also be found within The Five Stairsteps: a family of soul singers who had enjoyed a sizable hit in 1970 with 'O-o-h Child'. Billy Preston served as producer of their *2nd Resurrection* album, and bassist Keni Burke – determined to use Dark Horse as his springboard for solo success – wrote a note of thanks to Harrison on his eponymous 1977 debut.

As Harrison was still under contract to EMI, he was currently unable to release an album on his label, but that didn't stop him from writing an album. Like *The White Album* in the 1960s, the decision to record an album had functional as well as artistic reasons. By putting out the album, he was extricating himself from EMI: the record label to which he owed one more record. For the first time in his career, he chose to record an album outside England, and for someone who enjoyed their home comforts as much as Harrison did (*Living In The Material World* and *Dark Horse* were both written at Friar Park), this was a curious decision to make. There were challenges Harrison had to face – he ultimately decided to decamp to Los Angeles, where, lured by the lights of Hollywood, he began wandering the streets searching for distractions.

While his habits weren't as ominous as the alcohol addiction Ringo Starr would pick up; he was nonetheless falling victim to some of his excesses. 'I had been to a Los Angeles club – ended up in the back room with a lot of grey-haired naughty people, and I was depressed by what I saw going on there', he ruefully wrote in *I Me Mine*, no doubt concerned about the direction his life was heading in. Bassist Klaus Voorman had a similar opinion, describing this particular era as a 'terrible time'. 'I think there was a lot of cocaine going around, and that's when I got out of the picture', he told Simon Leng. 'I didn't want to get into that. I didn't like his frame of mind when he was doing this album. I don't play on it too much. The whole L.A. scene turned me off from playing sessions. I realised that it was the whole Hollywood thing – the problem was that if you wanted to stay in that scene, you had to hang out with those people and go and do the clubs. It wasn't me at all. George was in it too far at the time, and it was a good step of his to get out of it'.

It would take Harrison some time to face up to his drinking problem, but he did give some frank interviews on the subject: 'I wasn't ready to join Alcoholics Anonymous or anything – I don't think I was that far gone – but I could put back a bottle of brandy occasionally, plus all the other naughty things that fly around. I just went on a binge, went on the road, all that sort of thing, until it got to the point where I had no voice and almost nobody at times. Then I met Olivia, and it all worked out fine'.

Although his life was becoming increasingly complicated, the material itself was becoming more accessible, and whatever divergences threatened his personal life, did not affect the sound or the scope of the finished album. Despite his frantic antics, Harrison nonetheless cobbled together an album of excitement, resolution, vulnerability and possibility. Incredibly well-produced and performed with tremendous power, the album represented an incredible return-to-form for the musician. Gone were the extended displays of slide guitar, and much of the emphasis was being put on the keyboards. Considering the many Beatles songs he'd written on the piano (not forgetting his adept use of synthesizers on *Electronic Sound* and *Abbey Road*), it wasn't too radical a shift, but it did offer listeners a chance to experience a different side to his trajectory. But when he did play slide guitar (much as he did on the excoriating 'This Guitar (Can't Keep From Crying)'), the result sounded exhilarating, engaging, and certainly unique amidst the album's more-carefully-considered textures.

What you experience on *Extra Texture (Read All About It)* is an artist eager to return to the studio and making no concessions for his ambitions. There was no reason for him to return to the stage, so he didn't have to worry about how he was going to translate it from one medium to the next. It's a hard thing for any artist to make an album, but *Extra Texture* felt like the greatest victory of any in the Harrison canon: him somehow recovering from the disastrous tour, before charging into the ever-changing musical landscape, and demonstrating that the most (supposedly) stubborn Beatle could let loose and play. The album could've very easily spelled disaster in more ways than one, and yet it luxuriates in confidence.

If the album has a theme, it's rediscovery, even re-birth; the sound of a man undergoing a divorce, celebrating the best parts of his life, and looking to mend the mistakes he made on his journey to acceptance. *Extra Texture* certainly sounds like the cry of a fragile soul, torn between the cruel reviews that stripped away the integrity of his art and the desire to salvage himself within the soul genre that was slowly reviving his creative muse. But although the album sounded fresher and richer than anything he'd produced since 1970, the songs felt more unassuming, more apprehensive and less sure of themselves; the feistiness and passion that had lit the preceding albums, less evident here.

In a carousel of drugs, divergences and disputes, Harrison came to regard the album as the least satisfactory he'd completed since *All Things Must Pass* but caught between the soaring horns and the chiming guitars, his reticence and vulnerability makes for arresting listening. And caught between the towering opening track ('You') and the Beatle throwback ('This Guitar (Can't Keep From Crying)') comes 'The Answer's At The End': one of the most detailed – and certainly most distinguished – vocal performances of his career. *Extra Texture (Read All About It)* truly is Harrison's most underappreciated masterpiece, showcasing his desire to piece himself back together after a long and arduous year. Searching the carvings that surrounded his garden gates, Harrison happened upon an inscription written by Frank Crisp himself:

Scan not a friend with a microscopic glass
You know his faults, now let his foibles pass
Life is one long enigma, my friend
So read on, read on, the answer's at the end

Fuelled by the message that welcomed him home, Harrison used the verse on 'The Answer's At The End', encouraging him to complete the track and commemorate the microscopist for the public. Harrison's school friend Paul McCartney was enjoying the type of success that could be measured outside of a magnifying glass, and following the release of the riveting *Venus and Mars*, he shouldered a limelight that was once divided between four individual Beatles. Although Harrison never said it out loud, he must've felt relieved enough by McCartney's success to carve out his own path, safe in the knowledge that with the world focussing on *that* Beatle, Harrison was free to do anything he wanted. It's as if he looked hard at himself and decided to alter some of the aspects of his trajectory.

Rather than return to the harder-edged production style of *Dark Horse*, *Extra Texture* has a lighter, more feminine quality; much of the work is played on keyboards as opposed to guitar. What few slide guitars are heard ('This Guitar (Can't Keep From Crying)', 'Tired Of Midnight Blue') are sparse: the majority of the instrumental passages performed on synthesizer and strings.

In stark contrast to the albums that preceded it, there are no religious canticles to be heard. Instead, the album has a more allegorical feel, pivoting from the agile to the absonant. Like The Beatles before him, Harrison could be spurred into creative epiphany during times of great upheaval, and no matter how he felt about himself during this period, his songs sounded electrifying, tinged as they were with drama, density and feeling. Like the writer himself, the album delved into extremes. There are moments of extraordinary lyrical beauty, followed by portraits of raw, unvarnished nerves. There are pieces of explosive, uncontrollable anger, and happier moments of quiet reflection. Somewhere between the recording outtakes and retakes, Harrison remembered the value of laughter, and the album ends on the first unabashedly-comic number since the days of 'I Dig Love' and 'Thanks For The Pepperoni'. As a statement, there was greater value to the album than he might have realised in 1975 – his work was beginning to lighten up, and now he was entering into more polished – and certainly more commercial – territories. From now on, his work continued to get brighter, culminating in the near-perfect pop sound of his eponymous album at the close of the decade.

As a coping strategy, he likened his rapid rise to fame and celebrity status to a tawdry western, devoid of irony or context: 'It used to be a joke on the American teenage movie scene. John would say in his American accent, 'Where are we going boys?', and we would say, 'To the top, Johnny!''. He needed humour to keep himself afloat, especially as he measured his art against the records that were the soundtrack to his younger days in Liverpool.

Extra Texture (Read All About It) can be viewed as Harrison's pinnacle as a sound artist – a striking pillar of work that's every bit as impressive (but less explosive) than the production style Spector tailored for *All*

Things Must Pass. Ronnie Spector's presence acknowledges the influence The Ronettes had on Harrison's music, and the singer's shrill voice can be heard rising against guitars, drums and saxophones. Klaus Voorman drops in to play bass on 'World Of Stone', creating the sort of hypnotic backdrop that had long been Manfred Mann's trademark: his every note positioned to focus the track, particularly in the context of a barrelling piano spiralling in every direction but forwards. The song ricochets from slow to quick, as if recreating the confusion that existed within the words. Depending on your persuasion, the song either espoused the virtues of – or apologised for – the spiritual apotheosis that made up much of *Dark Horse*. But *all* agree that it's a song of warning that cautions listeners against the darker elements of hero worship. And as if vacating himself from the soapbox he'd long chanted from, Harrison was recognising the value of disagreement in the world he'd helped bring colour to. It seemed that being a Beatle didn't halt the ageing process, and like his listeners before him, he still had 'Such a long, long way to go'. The lack of spiritual message made *Extra Texture* a less-incendiary artistic statement than its immediate predecessor, but there was no shortage of emotion heard on the album. Like the writer, the album delved in extremes, but at least he was expressing himself with more style.

From now on, Harrison's work continued to get brighter, culminating in the pop-heavy *Cloud Nine* album in 1987. Under Jeff Lynne's supervision, Harrison completed a tasty – albeit lightweight – album that did much to revive his commercial tidings in the US. But there was no denying the fact that *Cloud Nine* was the slightest album of his career, lacking either the grit or the gallows humour of his 1970s output. *Extra Texture (Read All About It)* came out just as Harrison was well-and-truly getting recognised as a composer. America's 'Sister Golden Hair' (produced by The Beatles' very own George Martin) featured a massed vocal sound, much as Harrison had created on 'My Sweet Lord', while Jimmy Page's 'The Rain Song' bore a tidy tip of the hat to 'Something', after he was spurred into action when he heard the former Beatle had criticised Led Zeppelin for their lack of ballads. Even Lennon was taking notice – Nobody Loves You (When You're Down and Out)' bristled under the weight of a sweeping slide guitar solo that sounded haughty, quixotic and Harrison-esque.

A certain freedom is evident on 'Grey Cloudy Lies': an energetic blend of instruments that demonstrates the guitarist's determination to showcase his adept knowledge of keyboards. Plunging listeners into a world of ambience and pensiveness, the song is cut from an entirely different cloth to more propulsive 'This Guitar(Can't Keep From Crying)', and demonstrated his liberated vocal. Jumping to the occasion, 'You' has a gigantic drum and saxophone sound, but the attention never diverts from Harrison's effervescent vocal. The power and wild tempestuousness more than made up for Harrison's limited range, but boy does he go for the chorus, aching for the body he is sure to make passionate love to. Backed by Ronnie Spector's ghostly harmony, Harrison was in good stead and the vocal performance for 'You' ranks among the best of his career.

After the soaring salvo of saxophones, 'The Answer's At The End' quietens the album with a deeply lyrical treatise on self-reflection. Purportedly inspired by an inscription found at Friar's Park, the pastoral ballad is as much an effort in self-restraint as it's meant for the audiences who appreciated the more folk-oriented songs in his wheelhouse. 'Don't be so hard on the ones that you need', he sings: the aphorism personal, universal and angular. Behind the vocal comes David Foster's string arrangement: the violins caught in the middle of the rising passion. Suddenly, the slide appears, bristling with fire, and the strings respond with urgency, obedience and anticipation.

Furthering the comedy, Harrison included a picture of himself, complete with the caption 'OHNOTHIMAGEN'. And then there were the musicians who did not contribute to the record: 'Danny Kootch doesn't appear on this record. Also not appearing on this record: Derek Taylor, Peter Sellers, Chuck Trammell, Dino Airall, Eric Idle, Dennis Killeen and Emil Richards'. Considering their recent fallout, he might as well have added John Lennon's name to the mix!

Harrison may have appeared glib on the album cover, but he spoke more sincerely in public, offering generous answers to questions he thought deserved them. And though he was happy to single out those who had not performed on the record, he was also more than happy to recognise the conceptual contributions gifted to him by those who did. Harrison explained in a radio interview: 'One of the guys who played bass on some of the tracks was just sitting with me as I was overdubbing something, and we were talking about something. And he said 'texture', and at the same time as I said 'extra', and that was it. It just became one of those... the flow, you know, the words 'extra texture', at the time it seemed funny. *Extra Texture (Read All About It)*. It was going to be called *OHNOTHIMAGEN*, which is actually the subtitle'. Even more deliciously, the album featured a picture of an apple devoured to the core. Considering Harrison's wickedly-dark sense of humour, the apple seemed to suggest that the label had lost much of its essence, leaving only the bare remains behind. The album is rich in scope, yet there's nothing portentous about the saxophone-heavy 'You', nor is there anything insidious about the acidic 'This Guitar (Can't Keep From Crying)'. What's remarkable about *Extra Texture* is how joyous it sounds: written in the aftermath of a tumultuous tour. More importantly, it holds a new type of serenity and one that stemmed more from the genre of soul, as opposed to the soul-baring lyrics of its immediate predecessor. *Extra Texture* was typical of Harrison, who faced that most fearful of existential crises with unflinching defiance and unflappable good humour. The album came out at a time when certain quarters of the music press were writing the Beatle guitarist off as stodgy and unchanging. How wonderful it must've been for listeners to hear the vibrant and virile 'Can't Stop Thinking About You' for the first time in 1975, and think how exciting it must've been to hear Harrison tinkering with the pop formula, as he does so gleefully on 'A Bit More Of You'. And on 'This Guitar (Can't Keep From Crying)', Harrison made it clear how little he valued the opinions of the journalists who nearly pushed him over the edge:

While you attack, create offence
I'll put it down to your ignorance
But this guitar, it can't keep from crying
This guitar can't keep from crying

The album closes not with a thunderous rocker but a jolly good laugh. 'His Name Is Legs (Ladies And Gentlemen)' – all five minutes and 46 seconds of it – proved to be an accomplished hybrid, combining the guitarist's sense of melody with the The Bonzo Dog Doo-Dah Band's penchant for zaniness. 'Legs' Larry Smith – nominally the drummer for the Bonzos – takes the second lead on the track, relishing the opportunity to play such a wacky lyric on a rock album. The silliest song Harrison had yet produced, 'His Name Is Legs', also found the guitarist sharing vocal duties for the second time on the album. But unlike Ronnie Spector's spectral and shrill harmony line, 'Legs' Larry Smith delivered his lines in a jocular manner that recalled the jaunty, jokey choruses typically heralded by The Scaffold. He'd grown up around comedy rock, and Harrison recognised that the best way to sell this particular number was to invite the drummer from The Bonzo Dog Doo-Dah Band on as co-host. Harrison told rock writer Paul Gambaccini:

'Even if you see (the words) written down, you still won't understand them. It's the craziest song, both lyrically and musically'.

Having recorded the basic rhythm track during the *Dark Horse* sessions, Harrison now finished the track by compiling the necessary overdubs. As ever, he was happy to allow the musicians to come up with their own parts: a courtesy he extended to Smith. Portraying himself as a gentleman of some repute, Smith improvised many of the lines that made it onto the track. It was one of the more-surreal numbers in Harrison's catalogue, one of the most original too, and Smith felt flattered to be involved in the song: 'In the main hall there was a Steinway grand piano, and he burst in, sat down, gave me a nod, and started playing this song', Smith recalled. 'I was greatly touched by the whole thing'. The song – like much of the album – sits *uniquely* in Harrison's canon and holds a flavour entirely of its own.

For this listener, *Extra Texture* is Harrison's most satisfying studio album after the unimpeachable *All Things Must Pass*. Musically, *Extra Texture* was a transitional album for him, developing on the prior album's funk and soul influences while also developing a newer, more-contemporary direction through his use of synthesizers and brass. And in its own charming way, the album effectively divides the decade by moving away from the spiritual yearning of the first three albums and gliding into more mature radio-friendly territory. And he produced it all on one vinyl!

This trend would culminate in the self-titled album: one that was perfectly and unapologetically comfortable in its skin as an example of trendy art-pop. Following his most impenetrable work (*Dark Horse*) with a lushly-produced album was the only way Harrison could move forward with his art, and although his younger self might've found this change of pace difficult to countenance, it did show emotional growth on the part of a guitar player who was known – and applauded – for his stubbornness. Yet *Extra Texture* also marked a halfway point between the longing heard on *All Things Must Pass*, and the more family-oriented ethos of *George Harrison*. Between these pillars, Harrison witnessed tremendous change in his personal life – beginning the decade as one of the eminent songwriters of his generation, and closing it as one of England's burgeoning film producers. Reluctantly or otherwise, he proved himself as one of the 1970s great polymaths. And like 10cc's Kevin Godley, Harrison showed there were many sides to play in the rock pantheon. Caught in the change of life, Harrison had similarly grown as a person, and with the breakdown of one marriage, he was preparing himself for a newer, longer-lasting relationship.

1976: Lord, He's Fine

Harrison's spiritual focus was important to him, and influenced him for most of his adult life. It didn't matter whether he was married or unmarried, prosperous or perspicacious, wealthy or strapped. He found it was important to remind himself of his fallibility in the face of great power. 'He realised that this fame business – and I'll use the technical philosophical term here – complete bullshit', said Eric Idle in the eulogy at Harrison's funeral, 'And he turned to find beauty and truth and meaning in life, and, more extraordinarily, found it'.

At long last, Harrison's contract with EMI had expired, and he was now free to release his work on the label he founded. Although in 1973 he claimed he didn't care whether the world took any notice of him, in 1976, he was willing to return to the spotlight to showcase his tunefulness, tenderness and unflappable nature on the busiest press campaign of his life. As it happened, his interviews eclipsed his material. While *Thirty Three & 1/3* sounded hesitant, self-conscious and derivative, his demeanour seemed candid, colourful, and prone to a hilarious quip. He frequently cackled on television, and he seemed happy with his appearance, his clean-shaven face making him appear younger and arguably fresher, looking better than he had in some time. With his tousled hair and penchant for dry, droll one-liners, Harrison had acquired the persona of a charismatic – if slightly silky – raconteur. He brushed off questions about mortality with cheerful candour and compassion. He responded generously to questions asked about The Beatles and didn't seem eager to denigrate their ongoing influence. He played it cool.

Perhaps mindful of his incendiary public remarks in 1974, Harrison opted to give a more-nuanced answer for why The Beatles weren´t interested in reuniting. It wasn´t because of Paul McCartney´s domineering attitude, nor was it because of the apathy John Lennon showed for his work. It was simply because his tenure in The Beatles reminded him of his 'school' days: 'The four of us are so tied up with our own lives, and it's been eight years since we split. And time goes so fast'. To soften the blow, he did add that it wasn´t entirely beyond the realms of possibility, but it would take something more substantial than a cheque to reunite four disparate individual artists in one room together: 'We wouldn't stick together because somebody had put an ad in the paper putting us on the spot'. Harrison downplayed any suggestions that the band would reunite, but he seemed happier reflecting on their achievements than he had been on the Dark Horse tour.

During one memorable television interview, Harrison was presented with a clip of The Beatles performing 'This Boy' onstage. Clearly moved by the performance, he cackled uproariously as he watched Lennon and McCartney peer uneasily into the camera. Yes. He laughed. But Harrison was noticeably impressed with the glistening harmonies and professional stagecraft in the footage of three men still in their early-20s. Unlike McCartney – then excelling as a live performer – Harrison didn't seem eager to return to the stages (He still bore the scars from 1974), but he cheerfully indulged audiences in a stroll down memory lane: 'I suppose back in the '60s I thought... I gave meself till about 36', he quipped. 'So, still got a couple of years. But I think probably around 37 or 38, I feel then I could stop'. Asked in the same interview if he'd ever seen himself in another position, the guitarist dryly replied, 'Recently, I've been more of a lawyer'.

There have been times in recent history that when they sense a suit, they act on it privately and professionally. Take Monty Python's Neil Innes, who noted the similarity between his piano ditty 'How Sweet To Be Idiot' and the 1990s Oasis composition 'Whatever': 'I thought, 'Well, I better ring up EMI about it' because they'd published it. Immediately they said, 'We're on it! We're already on it!'. Apparently, they settled out of court. '(Oasis) put their hands up and gave me a quarter of 'Whatever.' It goes to EMI, where it's then divided 50/50 between EMI and me'. Harrison found himself in a similar situation with ' My Sweet Lord', which many felt resembled the tune to 'He's So Fine'.

No stranger to gentlemanly handshakes, Harrison would've probably met up with Ronnie Mack, the composer of 'He's So Fine', if he'd still been alive, but instead, Harrison had to counter against a corporation acting on their client's best interests. Together, The Beatles chose to collectively sue Allen Klein: a move that hurt Harrison in the long run. Having advised Harrison to purchase Bright Tunes (the publishing company that owned the rights to 'He's So Fine'), Klein opted to outbid Harrison, his former client for the publishing company. It was obviously a pointed move, but Klein ultimately coughed up the $587,000 needed to buy 'He's So Fine' in 1978. It's tempting to imagine that Klein viewed the damages Harrison was required to pay as compensation for the way Harrison, Lennon and Starr had turned their backs on him. But Klein also wouldn't have survived the length of time he put into the music industry if he wasn't prepared to throw a punch every now and then. He was mercenary and managerial but also prepared to seek vengeance when it suited him. And Harrison had unwittingly made it onto his list of targets (a bittersweet collection of names that would also include The Verve's Richard Ashcroft in the late-1990s). But Klein's duplicity was noted, and on 19 February 1981, the court ruled that Harrison pay Klein $587,000 – the amount the manager had spent on the track that underserved much of Harrison's caché – and in return, the ex-Beatle could have the rights to 'He's So Fine'.

Influence is sometimes obvious, but most songwriters make great effort to disguise the work that may have been the blueprint for theirs. The Beatles themselves were swayed by songwriters who inspired them, but through the guidance of George Martin, they tended to paint over any obvious tells, so the music sounded fresh, vital and original. Harrison – who had to be convinced to release 'My Sweet Lord' as a single – had rarely shown anything but original thought in his writing, and he maintained that the incident was an accidental oversight for the rest of his life. It was an emotional argument, but one that did not hold up in court. Standing in court, Harrison demonstrated a professional candour – eager as ever to not allow the world press to enter into his personal life without his permission. Harrison admitted in *I Me Mine*: 'I wasn't consciously aware of the similarity between 'He's So Fine' and 'My Sweet Lord' when I wrote the song, as it was more improvised and not so fixed. Although when my version of the song came out and started to get a lot of airplay, people started talking about it, and it was then I thought, 'Why didn't I realize?'. It would have been very easy to change a note here or there, and not affect the feeling of the record'.

Harrison had only agreed to issue 'My Sweet Lord' as a single on the advice of those he trusted, but it's doubtful anyone predicted that it would quickly establish itself as one of the most memorable singles of the era. But the victory was short-lived because Bright Tunes – a seminal music publishing company – had decided that the similarities between Harrison's anthem and Ronnie Mack's 'He's So Fine' were too great to ignore. Acting on the late Mack's behalf, Bright Tunes decided to sue Harrison, citing the 'I really want to see you' line as grounds to bring the songwriter to court. It didn't help that both song titles held three syllables in their song titles-not forgetting the fact that both songs featured lush, expansive backing vocals that featured prominently on their recordings. Yes, there was a resemblance, but Harrison wasn't the first songwriter

– not even the first Beatle – to lean on an influence, consciously or subconsciously. Trumpeter Humphrey Lyttelton's playing was felt on 'Lady Madonna', Chuck Berry had influenced 'Come Together', and then there was the matter of Led Zeppelin – a band many pencilled as The Beatles logical successors – who had issued two albums with moments of dubious authorship. Was Harrison unlucky? Ringo Starr certainly thought so: 'There's no doubt that the tune is similar, but how many songs have been written with other melodies in mind? George's version is much heavier than The Chiffons – he might have done it with the original in the back of his mind, but he's just very unlucky that someone wanted to make it a test case in court'. John Lennon was much less charitable with his words in 1980: 'George could have changed a few bars in that song and nobody could have ever touched him, but he just let it go and paid the price. Maybe he thought God would just sort of let him off'. Considering how heavily Lennon had leaned on past works for 'Come Together' and 'Happy Xmas (War Is Over)', there was a lack of self-awareness in his comment, but he did make a valid point about how pious Harrison had become since the mid-1960s. The key issue for Lennon and others was that the crusade Harrison had involuntarily set himself on (or, more accurately, the crusade that had landed in his lap during the recording of The Beatles' most-problematic album, *Let It Be*) seemed to echo the figures The Beatles had spent much of their time rebelling against. But then again, maybe his bandmates should shoulder some of the blame. Had The Beatles encouraged Harrison to write tunes from the beginning of their career, giving him the chance to match Lennon and McCartney on every record, perhaps Harrison's interest in spiritual rock (and more importantly, an escape from his growing resentment of the band) would not have been as feverish as it would manifest itself in 1970. Then again, the world would've been robbed of 'My Sweet Lord': a hymn that blew even the most hardened of religious sceptics (Lennon included) away with its sincerity. From great anger came a work of tremendous beauty, and though the tune may not have been original, the lyric and sentiment definitely were. And although it took a certain amount of courage to denounce the sanctity of religion in the 1970s, it was arguably harder to make a case for it, especially one with such a dazzling sound. The song has outlived both its writer (Harrison) and co-producer (Phil Spector), and will likely continue to inspire songwriters long after you and I have completed our earthly journeys. For Harrison, the humiliation was temporary, but the legacy of the song is eternal.

Still preoccupied with what he considered to be a petty affair, Harrison was spending more time ruminating on his past failings than he was creating new and more-invigorating art that would elevate his status. Yet just as his life was slipping into near-pastiche, he rose to the occasion with 'This Song': a blinding piece that suggested how his life and art could progress if he wanted it to. To symbolise that the acidity was genuine, Harrison decided to direct a video set in a courtroom, equipped with silly mallets, moustaches and wigs. And Eric Idle recorded a series of silly, scintillating falsettos that recalled the many women characters in *Monty Python's Flying Circus*. In one almost tantric opening address, Harrison lets out years of pent-up frustrations in a deliciously dark piece of writing. Berating the legal departments who were determined to monetise the value of his intellectual property, Harrison decided to meet what he perceived as idiocy with a comedy number of his own. Through a suitably-bombastic opening, the cascading instruments make way for a fiery opening line, as Harrison openly mocks the men he deemed unqualified to comment on the originality of his work: 'I did record 'This Song', which was kind of a comment about the situation. The thing that really disappoints me is when you have a relationship with one person, and they turn out to betray you. Because the whole story of 'My Sweet Lord' is based upon this fellow Allen Klein who managed the Beatles from about 1968 or '69 through until 1973. When they issued a complaint about 'My Sweet Lord', he was my business manager'.

Although the court cases were painful to sit through, Harrison likely wrote them off as an added fixture to the great tapestry that was unravelling around him. Darkness, he reasoned, was as essential to the density of his personal narrative as the good times were. In her best efforts to explain the duology, Olivia Arias came up with a comparison of her own: 'He had karma to work out. [He} wasn't going to come back and be bad. He was going to be good and bad and loving and angry and everything all at once. You know, if someone said to you, 'Okay, you can go through your life and you can have everything in five lifetimes, or you can have a really intense one and have it in one, and then you can go and be liberated', he would have said 'Give me the one, I'm not coming back''.

Ringo Starr – at one time the most popular of the solo Beatles – had released a compilation of his jauntiest material, and Lennon had also unveiled *Shaved Fish*: a compendium of solo singles that had graced the US airwaves. McCartney would hold out on releasing a hits package until 1978, but *Wings Greatest* was the tidiest of all, demonstrating the bassist's pop flair and penchant for anthemic rock. Harrison, on the other hand, found himself in the unenviable position of releasing a greatest hits compilation album that placed some of his Beatles songs among his more-personal 1970s work. Considering the calibre of the Beatle songs 'If I Needed Someone', 'Something' and 'For You Blue', the album was a more-than-pleasant experience, but Harrison did not take kindly to the decision: 'There was really a lot of good songs they could have used of me separately. Solo songs. I don't see why they didn't do that'. If the writer felt unhappy with the product, it did little to turn off the critics. *Billboard* considered it an album full of 'memorably beautiful hits', while *Melody Maker*'s Ray Coleman praised Harrison's individual artistry and 'creative musical company'. Harrison's critical cachet was on the rise and riding on the wave of Beatles nostalgia, the 13-song set showed his talents both inside and outside The Fabs.

Thirty Three & 1/3

Personnel:
George Harrison: vocals, electric and acoustic guitar, synthesizer, percussion
Tom Scott: saxophone, flute, Lyricon
Billy Preston: piano, organ, synthesizer
Richard Tee: piano, organ, Fender Rhodes
David Foster: Fender Rhodes, clavinet
Gary Wright: keyboards
Emil Richards: marimba
Willie Weeks: bass
Alvin Taylor: drums
Record label: Dark Horse
Recorded 24 May-13 September 1976, at FPSHOT, Oxfordshire
Produced by George Harrison and Tom Scott
Release dates: UK: 19 November 1976, US: 24 November 1976
Chart placings: UK: 35, US: 11
Running Time: 39:15

For now, Harrison had an album to complete. But the recording was halted after he contracted hepatitis C, so he took time off to undergo acupuncture and other non-traditional remedies. The rest did him good, and he returned to the recordings with renewed vigour. Wisely, he decided not to take on all production work and asked Tom Scott to help him. If Scott expected a co-producing credit, he was set to be disappointed, as he was invariably credited for 'assistance'. But it was a step forward and was the first time that the musician held some sway over the content since the days of Mr. Spector. Even more miraculous than Harrison's recovery from hepatitis C was his decision to quit drinking. The two events weren't unrelated, leading Harrison to quip, 'I needed the hepatitis to quit drinking'.

And then there was Olivia Arias: very much the soulmate he'd spent a lifetime searching for. They shared an interest in vegetarianism, eastern philosophy and gardening, but they complemented each other in other ways. He made her laugh, she made him smile, and they deeply trusted one another. Following her lead, Harrison explored natural remedies (à la acupuncture), and he paid tribute to her presence in his songs.

Thirty Three & 1/3 is an album that fans had come to expect from the man they'd followed for more than half a decade. But there's something more complacent about the work. It ultimately lacks the sense of adventure of the album that preceded it, nor does he enjoy the sanctity of his environment as he would on the brilliant *George Harrison* album in 1979. This is not to say that *Thirty Three & 1/3* doesn't have its moments (The complacency that kicked into his work in the 1980s had yet to rear its head), but it's strangely pedestrian for a man who was determined to stand out at all junctures. And for a composer/person of Harrison´s stature to release anything that would be considered common was disappointing. Where *Extra Texture (Read All About It)* was a daringly-structured document of creativity – replete with knowing remarks and blinding moments of instrumental flourish – *Thirty Three & 1/3* sounded like an instruction manual, occasionally deviating from the formula to let out a whimsical 'twoo': a term lifted from Mel Brooks' then-latest comedy *Blazing Saddles.*

But for all the album's failings (It exhibited more negatives than positives), it deserves some credit for asserting Harrison's individuality, especially after suffering the ignominy of a lawsuit. Rather than let it grind him down, Harrison re-emerged with one of the most distinguished songs of his career, fashioning an acidity that felt in keeping with his life's work. Many of his Beatles songs ('Think For Yourself', 'Taxman', 'Piggies') were written about what he perceived as societal failings, but 'This Song' goes one further, openly ridiculing the judicial system that monetised his art according to their wishes. If the album has a masterpiece, this is the one: encapsulating a dark wit that had long been part of Harrison's makeup.

Paramahansa Yogananda's influence rears its head, especially on 'It's What You Value' – Harrison's rumination on a world where currency and trade are as relevant as the soul permits it to be. Inspired by Jim Keltner's form of payment for the Dark Horse tour, 'It's What You Value' could also have been read as Harrison's public admission of his passion for vehicles. The drummer had declined a fee but asked that the Beatle buy him a new car. Harrison was sufficiently amused by the request to turn it into a comic ditty. He probably shouldn't have bothered! Cars were becoming a more integral part of the rock star image: Queen's Roger Taylor seemed to prefer them to women! Harrison was also becoming more drawn to the wonders of the wheel, and he was often spotted driving around Friar Park in a splashy car of his choice. He felt driving was meditative, and he later compared the art of driving to the practices he learned in Marrakesh: 'I know that racing is, to a lot of people, dopey, maybe from a spiritual point of view. Motor cars – polluters, killers, maimers, noisemakers. Good racing though involves heightened awareness for the competitors...'. Keltner's declining of monetary payment for the Dark Horse tour, stayed with Harrison long enough to put it to tape in 1976. Sadly, the lyric doesn't do justice to the concept, and the end result is a lazy rehash of vehicular references, driven by a pounding piano line. Personally, I'd stick to Queen's 'I'm In Love With My Car' if I were you, or try Gary Numan's 'Cars', if you're into that kind of thing!

The strangely moving 'Dear One' is much more successful, representing a powerful yet somehow muted statement. Harrison played many of the synthesizers heard on 'Dear One'. There – hidden behind a distinctly fresh-sounding record – his lyric stemmed from a text first published in the 1940s:

My spirit sings to you now
Creation stands at your feet
My feelings call to you now
Dear One I love -a-you

Then there's 'Crackerbox Palace': an anodyne tune better remembered for its accompanying video. Detailing the escapades of a man caught in arrested development, the song carries the narrator from his early days in the pram to the adult decisions he has to make daily. It sounded promising on paper, but, sadly, the choppy guitar, propulsive bass and swampy synthesizer drowned out many of the song's more interesting nuances. Yet bearing in mind the degree of flippancy evinced on the track, it made sense that a Python should direct the promotional video.

Eric Idle's memorable video shows Harrison at his wildest, weirdest and most-downright wacky. The clean-shaven Beatle jumps out of a pram just in time to sing his song before shaking his hands to the beat of a swallow taking flight. The camera turns on Harrison, cheekbones as sharp as razors, flaunting a hairstyle that made him appear five years younger. He looks strangely handsome, especially amongst the entourage of clowns that await him at his house. Olivia pops up, her arm wrapped around the upholstery, laced in a leather outfit that showcased her sylphlike body. The 'Crackerbox Palace' video is a glorious romp; silly and camp but presented in a manner that recalls those vaudeville routines of yore. And it restored Harrison to the place Richard Lester felt suited him nicely: the world of acting.

If Harrison had been hesitant to include Olivia in the *Extra Texture* narrative, he was now comfortable enough to welcome her into his work through mirth, melody and mantra. Her fingerprints are all over 'Learning How To Love You', guiding her partner's vocal through a sweet, lingering vocal performance. 'Beautiful Girl' – a thinly-sketched lyric written for Pattie in 1970 – now had greater weight. And 'True Love' – a Cole Porter standard repurposed for the album – had a truth that could only have sprung from a place of tremendous stability and comfort. As if furthering the point to its most visible place, Olivia stood by Harrison in the promotional videos from the period. 'True Love' was here reinterpreted to include a shuffling backbeat and features Harrison's trademark choppy – almost Hawaiian – guitar work. Past cover songs were instated to demonstrate his gratitude to some of the friends who'd made his life more complete ('If Not For You'), or to issue an indictment about the failures the institution of marriage had caused him ('Bye Bye Love'). There didn't seem to be any reason to include 'True Love' besides the fact that Harrison enjoyed the song so much, and it breezily earned its place on the album.

The album held another formidable opus in 'Learning How To Love You': a lovelorn ballad initially pencilled for trumpeter Herp Alpert. Beautifully produced and sung with tremendous passion, the song represented Harrison's penchant for narrative – a work equally as reliant on restraint and brute strength as it is about the lingering side-effects of infatuation. Python alumnus Eric Idle directed the video. 'I was fortunate that he was kind of a guru to me', Idle remembered. 'I mean, he was a pal, we got drunk, we did all sorts of wicked, naughty things and had a ball. But he was always saying, 'Well, don't forget you're gonna die'.

Driven by plodding drums and a wailing guitar hook, Harrison's incendiary 'See Yourself' was typically caustic fodder from the erstwhile Beatle, but it stemmed from the very band that he seemed happy to close out on. Atypically, Harrison rose to the defence of McCartney, sympathising with a predicament the bassist had found himself in. Harrison wrote: 'There was a big outcry with people saying (to McCartney), 'You should have said 'No!''. However wounded Harrison was by McCartney's decision to discuss his acid intake in 1967, the guitarist nonetheless felt greater disgust at the press who decorated their papers with gossip and general nonsense. In March 1969, Harrison endured an even more humiliating push when he was arrested for cannabis possession. 'They chose Paul's wedding day to come and do a raid on me, and to this day, I'm still having difficulty with my visa to America because of this fella', Harrison recalled, the fury still evident. But he found it in himself to channel this emotion on 'See Yourself': a feisty rock number that preached the virtues of honesty in a world dedicated to the currency of slander. Like most of the album, it was strong, but could've been stronger, particularly from a musical standpoint: though the lyric embodied anger, the backing was too staid to inflect that passion onto the audience (While we're talking about McCartney, the same could be said about his 'Angry': written as a riposte to what he considered uncivil behaviour from the British press. If there was any fury to be heard, it was wiped from the final mix).

Then there's 'Woman Don't You Cry For Me', which offers listeners the shot in the arm the album needs after such a long interlude of uninteresting material. Harrison's in fine form and his guitar has rarely sounded freer; wailing across a loose, lingering display of bass, keyboards and drums. Where once he played with little swagger or spontaneity, 'Woman Don't You Cry For Me' presents a complete 180, demonstrating the instrumentalist at his loosest, liveliest and most funky. Although he'd amassed a personal collection of James Brown records (Harrison adored Brown's smouldering rendition of 'Something'), Harrison had seldom aped the performer so openly and with such gravitas. It was the funkiest track he'd yet put to record.

But any hopes that the album would bring a complete change of direction are quickly abandoned on 'Pure Smokey'. Everything that's initially promising – but ultimately disappointing – about *Thirty Three & 1/3*, is encapsulated in 'Pure Smokey': an ill-thought-out reprise of musical motifs that had made up Harrison's past work. Somewhere within the haunting saxophone line comes the germ of an idea that should be developed into something more memorable and well-thought-out. But the track never takes off, showing scant interest in following the rock route the chorus points to, and neither does it stick to the stoic, more serene chant as evinced in the opening verse. Being neither aria nor anthem, the song is indicative of much of the record, neglecting to follow any one idea to the fullest. And that's the issue with the album – it's not the lack of ideas but the multitude of avenues that are left frustratingly unexplored.

According to drummer Alvin Taylor, the recording sessions were pleasant to engage in: 'It was like no other experience. We lived at the house and he was a perfect host, really concerned about your well-being, very considerate and extremely kind. He knew how to treat people and make them feel special. He did that with all the players. Most of the tracks were done in one, two or at most three takes. We worked from about 11 in the morning until four or five, recording the basic keyboards, guitar and bass parts'. A few early versions of the songs had been demoed as far back as 1970, but Harrison made sure to update the lyrics where needed to incorporate Arias. 'Beautiful Girl' had been floating in the background for years, and though the recorded version lacks the yearning of the 1970 vocal, it compensated with a selection of moving stanzas written about how grateful he was to have found love:

She has always been there
A lover needed for this soul to survive

Like many poets before him, Harrison's work was growing more pragmatic the older he got. And although 'Beautiful Girl' lacks the passion that made 'Something' such a bestseller, it carries the romanticism to the next level of maturity and logic. It wasn't one moment that made a successful pairing, but a mosaic of memories that binds a man and woman to that end point. As if eager to show this stage of maturity, Harrison demonstrated it as the album's title. Impish as ever, he couldn't resist adding '1/3', though the more intellectually inclined of Harrison's followers could attribute it to the work of Italian filmmaker Frederico Fellini. Cinema was growing larger on Harrison's radar, and he was enjoying more and more time watching films in a private screening room. Soon he'd make that transformative leap into filmmaking himself, and naturally, his first two collaborations would be with Eric Idle.

Thirty Three & 1/3 boasted Harrison at his most charming and handsome, but the material was mostly disappointing. It does have 'This Song' and 'Learning How To Love You': two sumptuous, layered anthems showing Harrison at his cleverest. But these two tracks aside, the album feels slight when measured against the four that preceded it. For all the brevity, buoyancy and shrill guitar fills, there's no getting over the fact that Harrison's fifth solo album lacks the intellectual ambition of his debut – or, for that matter, the crispness and self-confidence of *Extra Texture (Read All About It)*. None of the songs were as lyrical as 'The Light That Has Lighted The World'; none of the slide solos could match the passion of 'So Sad', and nowhere on the album was there the sense of adventure that had produced such deliriously inventive fodder as 'Living In The Material World', 'Hari's On Tour' and 'Maya Love.' In a canon that had shown a growth that was almost comparable to The Beatles themselves, there's no escaping the fact that *Thirty Three & 1/3* is lesser Harrison.

It seemed McCartney was the only solo Beatle still capable of creating and prospering, being equally as comfortable writing music-hall numbers ('You Gave Me The Answer') as he was inhabiting the proto-metal roar of 'Beware My Love'. Ringo Starr had been experiencing dwindling numbers since 1975 and had developed a relationship with alcohol that was arguably more damaging than any liaison Harrison may have enjoyed with cocaine. The dalliance (or 'miserable disease' as the drummer so eloquently pegged it) may have affected his songwriting abilities, and though the early albums *Ringo* and *Goodnight Vienna* had a spark that was easier to get into than Harrison's, 1976's *Ringo's Rotogravure* showed little of the bravado and none of the intelligence of his earlier output.

But like the 1973 eponymous album before it, *Ringo's Rotogravure* does have the distinction of including three songs written by Beatle songwriters. Sadly, they weren't very good. Purportedly retired from the public, Lennon's 'Cookin' (In The Kitchen of Love)' earmarked itself as the very type of ballad he flatly refused to sing in the band, while McCartney's whimsical 'Pure Gold' showed none of the ingenuity heard on the radio standards 'Listen To What The Man Said', 'Silly Love Songs' and 'Let 'Em In'. But whatever the quality, it was an act of loyalty, not charity, that drove the three men to continue writing for Starr long after they'd parted company. And though Harrison was unable to pen a number specifically for his friend and confidante, he nonetheless gave his blessing to the drummer to record a Harrison song, 'I'll Still Love You', he'd once offered to Ronnie Spector: 'It was one of those that I tried several times to record: Ronnie Spector – Phil's wife – had a go at it; Cilla Black also', Harrison recalled in 1979. 'We also did it with Leon Russell and his wife Mary, and in the end, Ringo recorded it.'

The above interview betrays a damning indictment – rather than watch a shrill vocalist of Spector's calibre complete the work, Harrison had to content himself with the rousing, ramshackle sing-along that was heard on an album that scarcely bothered the US charts. But rather than humiliate his friend in public (those venomous comments were spared for McCartney), Harrison resolved to settle matters diplomatically and legally. The matter, resolved out of court, was one Starr would remember with tremendous good humour in the late-1980s. He told TV presenter Michael Aspel: 'The last time George was angry with me was when he was suing me'. Harrison, who sat beside Starr in this interview, emerged from his seat with faux embarrassment, but the words – heard with damning effect – must've troubled him in retrospect. Caught in the confines of a court dispute that threatened both his finances and reputation, Harrison had now acted with similar impunity towards the very musician who had supported him so wholly in the 1960s. This action made him human, but it did sit at odds with the sentiment heard on 'This Song': Harrison's damning excoriation of the suits who had caused him great pain as a person, and had caused him to second-guess himself as an artist. But it happened at a time when Harrison was beginning to give the industry greater attention, so the action was less of a pop star caught in the hypocrisy of his words and more the result of a practitioner taking his life, religion and craft that bit less seriously.

For the first time on a Harrison album, Klaus Voorman didn't play on a single song. Once pegged as a shoo-in for McCartney (John Lennon once proclaimed, 'If you'd said that George, Ringo and John had an idea they might play a live show or two, then Klaus would be our man to play with us'), Voorman was becoming less integral to the three Beatles he'd maintained a professional relationship with for the best part of a decade. But he did contribute to *Ringo's Rotogravure*: the drummer's ill-conceived attempt to remodel himself on the disco artists parading all over Atlantic Studios. Whatever Voorman's efforts, the album floundered, and Starr found *himself* floundering in the sphere of rock. More successful were his efforts in cinema, as roles in *That'll Be The Day*, *Son of Dracula* and *Lisztomania* had proven, and Starr was arguably showing that there were other ways to celebrate being a Beatle.

Harrison, too, was reinventing himself as a comedy Beatle, as his appearance on *Saturday Night Live* had shown. On 26 April 1976, the show's producer Lorne Michaels appeared before the cameras to offer The Beatles $3000 to reform. It was a joke, and a very funny one, and Harrison responded to it on the programme, in a cameo, asking for his cheque. 'It's teensy', he replied, seemingly disappointed in the money Michaels was willing to part with. Starr would likely have tried to upstage Michaels (McCartney definitely would've), but Harrison played it straight, allowing the material to speak for itself. In his deadpan way, Harrison was very funny, and he could've very well continued in this role as a stand-up comedian. But instead, he was standing up for himself, and he channelled his inner comedian in front of an audience who were clearly lapping it up.

Harrison joined Paul Simon on *Saturday Night Live*, embellishing Simon's 'Homeward Bound' with an infectious vocal harmony that could only have stemmed from a place of tremendous friendship. There were no pyrotechnics or accompanying musicians, just two men on guitars, complementing each other's work. Simon sang harmony on 'Here Comes The Sun', and although the cover did not capture the professionalism of the Beatles original, there was a spontaneity to it that invited audiences to sing along. The men seemed to enjoy each other's work, and Harrison seemed content in himself, shifting from vocalist to side musician. Best of all, the performance highlighted his northern vowels, as was heard on 'Homeward Bound'. 'Every day's an endless dream', Harrison sang, before unveiling his inner Scouser on 'cigarettes and ma-gu-zines'. At Harrison's request, Simon granted permission for the release of their rendition of 'Homeward Bound' on the 1990 charity album *Nobody's Child: Romanian Angel Appeal.*

Harrison was an admirer of Simon's craft, and the pair had tremendous respect for the other, both as songwriters and men. Simon told Conan O'Brien: 'Amazing person, not just as a musician, but really very very open, kind, not – you know, just a certain percentage of him Beatles, and the rest just regular, interested in life, interested in the world, interested in the mind. Really a pleasure to hang out with him'.

1977 and 1978: 'Keep 'em Laughing As You Go...'

In 1977, Harrison made a curious remark: 'Look, I'd be willing, every time I write a song if somebody will have a computer and I can just play any new song into it, and the computer will say 'Sorry' or 'Okay'. The last thing I want to do is keep spending my life in court'. Deeply hurt by the 'My Sweet Lord' suit, his self-confidence was floundering, which was not an ideal state to be in when engaged in a process of intense focus and creativity. His most recent work was banal, pedestrian and uninteresting, and unlike the interviews he gave to promote *Thirty Three & 1/3*, his work lacked menace, bite and singular vision.

And yet, he was still more than capable of being creative, not least when it came to poking fun at the band that made him famous. 'In music terms, I sort of skived for 1977', he admitted two years later when talking to BBC Radio 1. 'I went on strike. I just went to the races, actually, to the motor racing. I was just really getting a bit fed up with the music business, to tell you the truth. I mean, it had been a long time being in it and, you know, I just felt like a break. So I took 1977 away from music, and I didn't actually write a tune during that year. I just sort of forgot all about music, went to the races, and then at the end of '77, I thought, 'God, I better start doing something''.

In the meantime, he focussed on other areas in his life. He was, after all, a man in love, and rather than waste time on activities that didn't engage his heart; he chose to focus on the relationship that brought colour to his life. But he clearly took the court case to heart and was probably beginning to second-guess himself as a writer.

Contrary to popular belief, it wasn't Lorne Michaels' urging that brought The Rutles together, but a segment that featured on BBC 2 sketch show *Rutland Weekend Television*. Based in England's smallest county, Eric Idle's sketch programme was a cabalistic showcase of music, mania and general good humour. 'It was made on a shoestring budget, and someone else was wearing the shoe', Idle told *Radio Times*. 'The studio is the same size as the weather forecast studio, and nearly as good...'. Harrison guested on the show, and Neil Innes – considered by many, including the creative cohorts, as the unofficial seventh Python – would drop in to perform pieces of his songcraft. Together, Idle and Innes concocted the idea of a group that was equal-parts pastiche and homage. Harrison duly appeared on *Rutland Weekend Television*, regaling audiences of 'My Sweet Lord''s opening bars before abandoning any semblance of familiarity for a bawdy tale of pirate ships and daylight robbery. When the presenter (played brilliantly by Idle) ran on to complain, Harrison simply turned to the camera to deliver that most infectious of grins. With his long wavy hair and ivory eyes, Harrison looked every bit the ragged bohemian he undoubtedly thought himself to be, and the song – jaunty and jocular in equal measure – closed the episode on a joyful high. And yet there's a knowing irony to the scene that must have appealed to the guitarist's dark sense of humour – no matter how personal the nature of the song was to him, he was forced to pander to the opening strains of a ballad that barely belonged to him. Whether or not Harrison was inclined to read so deeply about himself, it must've been liberating for him to mock the impresarios who made it their personal mission to inform their artists exactly what their artistic worth was valued at. And why were they so concerned with *treasure* when the shanties, skulls and crossbows were there to be enjoyed?

Rutland Weekend Television did not take off in America, but The Rutles – a band concocted by Idle and fronted by Neil Innes – did. Hosting an episode of *Saturday Night Live* in 1976, Idle pulled out a clip of The Rutles performing 'I Must Be In Love': a sprightly pop number that recalled the days when The Beatles wore moptops and matching shirts. And that's where Lorne Michaels stepped in. Sensing a feature was in the making, he encouraged Idle (and SNL director Gary Weis) to put together a mockumentary, and in doing so, beat the Spinal Tap guys by six years. Harrison was all for the project. Producer Gary Weis remembered: 'We were sitting around in Eric's kitchen one day, planning a sequence that really ripped into the mythology, and George looked up and said, 'We were The Beatles, you know!'. Then he shook his head and said, 'Aw, never mind'. I think he was the only one of The Beatles who really could see the irony of it all'. Indeed, Harrison offered Idle his copy of *The Long and Winding Road*: an unreleased documentary the band had been toying with. Always the most youthful-looking of the Python actors, Idle had no problem slotting into the costume of a Rutle, though he also portrayed a musicologist coming down from the effects of something stronger than tea, as well as a disgruntled reporter who was determined to solve the mystery behind the group. Yes, it read like a pastiche of *Citizen Kane*, but the end result was something much more inspiring – setting up every member of The Beatles or what the public perception of each character was. Tellingly, Harrison's character barely speaks, while Lennon's alter ego Ron Nasty speaks in riddles and rhymes that rarely add up to anything coherent.

The Rutles (OST)

Personnel:
Neil Innes: vocals, keyboards, guitar
Ollie Halsall: guitar, keyboards, vocals
Rikki Fataar: guitar, bass, sitar, tabla, vocals
John Halsey: percussion, vocals
Andy Brown: bass
John Altman: orchestral arrangements
Cliff Haines: piccolo trumpet
Record label: Warner Bros.
Release dates: UK and US: March 1978
Chart placings: UK: 12, US: 68
Running Time: 36:13

The Rutles: All You Need Is Cash is a deliciously-written film. Everywhere we turn, there are Beatle jokes, each one more knowing and biting than the one that preceded it. There's Mick Jagger, who remembers the girls chasing The Rutles on live television; Dan Ackroyd, cast as the cigarette-chomping, foot-stomping executive who once turned down the band, and then there's George Harrison, dressed in grey, every bit the square media person he'd spent his life creating. Across from Harrison stands Michael Palin, wearing a moustache eerily similar to the one worn by Beatles publicist Derek Taylor in 1968. And hungry as ever for the laugh, no matter how brutal the punchline, Harrison was filmed interviewing members of Hells Angels: the organisation he'd declared misunderstood by the general public. The Angel is played by Ronnie Wood – Harrison's one-time co-writer and a man who would later write about a game of wife-swap he enjoyed with the Beatle. But whatever his penchant for tittle-tattle, Wood – like Jagger – proved to be hysterical in a film that had John Lennon and Yoko Ono in stitches in the safety of their New York home.

Idle – Python's most accomplished mimic – plays a variety of characters and acted as the film's co-director, which made sense, considering how much he was investing into the project. Naturally, Idle played up the thumbs and smiles that journalists associated with McCartney, but there's never a sense that Idle is belittling the bassist's talents. Songwriter Neil Innes recalled: 'The way it worked was that Eric wrote stuff, and then I was covering the music bases and coming up with musical ideas. It was supposed to be a television station, so it wouldn't just be talking; you'd have to break it up. So it was my job to think up cheap musical ideas and song ideas. One of them was to do a spoof of *Hard Day's Night* because it was black and white, speeded up, four guys, four wigs, tight trousers, pointy shoes, running around a field. It's got to be cheap! It was a cheap joke!'.

Some of the tracks – especially the country-rock ballad 'It's Looking Good' – definitely felt like they were songs The Beatles would've released in their heyday, but listening to the songs now, they sound like the template for Britpop albums *Modern Life Is Rubbish (Blur)* and *(What's The Story) Morning Glory?* (Oasis). Innes did overstep on 'Get Up and Go', a hillbilly rocker that felt like it was leaning too heavily on 'Get Back'. As it happens, it was dropped from the vinyl upon release.

The gap between cinema and rock had been closing in recent times. Pete Townshend had written two rock operas that he intended to bring to the screen, and Frank Zappa – the most contrary composer in an industry of contrarians – took a crack at directing alongside Tony Palmer, in 1971 (He hired Ringo Starr to play the lead). And with *The Rutles: All You Need Is Cash*, Harrison witnessed two of his life passions being melded together. 'I have always, for the last few years anyway, felt film and music can really enhance each other to get a point out', he admitted in 1975, and he was impressed by the songs that were composed specifically for the work. Without the songs, the film would've been an above-average attempt to satirise The Beatles; with them, the film was something extra-special.

For all the rapier satire and knowing approach to songwriting, The Rutles (as the group of musicians called themselves) were an extraordinarily-tight outfit. Bandleader Innes had previously fronted The Bonzo Dog Doo-Dah Band, drummer John Halsey had performed on the Lou Reed classic *Transformer*, and then there was Ollie Halsall: a lead guitar player who had a profound influence on the work of XTC's Andy Partridge. The XTC frontman told *Popdose*: '(He) played such inventive runs, not your standard blues stash of things, or the standard blues licks that absolutely everybody was doing. Once I heard his guitar-playing, I was like, 'Oh, I need to be able to play like that!''. Halsall sang the more-whimsical material while Innes took on the rock numbers. Drummer John Halsey sang 'Living In Hope' in a style remarkably similar to Ringo Starr's, while 'Nevertheless' – a sitar piece written in the mould of Ravi Shankar – was performed by South African musician Ricky Fataar. Like Innes and Halsey, Fataar wound up playing his Rutle character in the film.

Eric Idle mimed to Halsall's vocals in the film, leading some to suspect that the Python sang on the record. Nonetheless, Idle's portrayal of Dirk McQuickley was merciless, capturing Paul McCartney at his most docile, doe-eyed and dapper. Innes told *Beatlefan* writer Ken Sharp: 'Paul had an album out at the same time as *The Rutles* came out and was forever saying 'No comment' about The Rutles. He had dinner at some award thing at the same table as Eric one night, and Eric said it was a little frosty'. In the same interview, Innes felt that Starr also held some reservations: '...after Leggy (Brian Epstein) dies, it's miserable. You feel, 'what a downer'. And so, it was a way of telling the story without downing the audience, skipping over the sad bits. So I think Ringo was too much reminded of the real breakup'.

More happily, Idle was told that Yoko Ono – commonly vilified in Beatle biopics – saw the irony behind the project. Idle admitted decades later: 'I thought, 'That's really good of Yoko to love it', because she's portrayed as Hitler's daughter!'. Unfortunately, those in the legal profession failed to see the funny side, and despite Harrison's involvement in the project – and Lennon's blessing of it – Innes found himself the recipient of a legal action which necessitated that the publishing royalties of the fourteen songs be siphoned off to Lennon and McCartney's Northern Songs: even for the Harrison and Starr parodies. It must've been galling for Harrison, who'd been forced to sit through something very similar, and he rallied around Innes. They remained good friends, and when The Rutles decided to record a follow-up album in the 1990s, Harrison gave the project his blessing. 'It's all part of the soup', he surmised.

Harrison's way of making stern, scathing remarks made him a natural to collaborate with The Rutles. Seven years had passed since leaving The Beatles, and unlike the more convivial Lennon, he was finding it harder to embrace the nostalgia the group had left behind. He was still eager to follow the importance of the present moment, and though he was asked to put seven Beatles compositions on *The Best of George Harrison*, it was not an act he pursued with great relish. Bewildered by *John, Paul, George, Ringo ... and Bert* – a rousing 1974 jukebox musical that premiered at The Everyman in Liverpool – Harrison withdrew his permission to use 'Here Comes The Sun'. For once, McCartney was in agreement, and he put the kibosh on a proposed film adaptation of the musical.

They may have agreed on the merits of a hackneyed musical, but McCartney was more reluctant to enjoy the concept of The Rutles. Coinciding with the release of Wings' *London Town* (a pastoral album that saw McCartney tackling much of the instrumentation, following the dismissal of guitarist Jimmy McCulloch), McCartney was bemused by the many journalists who focused their attention on the comedy rather than the Wings album. No doubt Harrison enjoyed McCartney's embarrassment, considering Harrison's dislike of promotional trails and how vividly he remembered the bassist's desire to cater to every fan, writer and manager. In later years, Innes sympathised with McCartney and offered *DangerousMinds* a mea culpa of sorts: ' I don't think Paul has any issues with me, or Ricky or John. We pretty much just did the music. I think a bit of teasing is okay if you do it in a 'nudge, nudge, wink, wink' way. But Eric did make quite a few cheap shots in the movie – maybe that's why Paul was a bit chilly and didn't see the funny side of it'. Invariably, McCartney's views softened on the project, which Idle was happy to admit in 2018. And in their own idiosyncratic way, The Rutles helped Harrison to forgive himself and his former bandmates: 'The Rutles sort of liberated me from The Beatles in a way. It was the only thing I saw of those Beatles television shows they made. It was actually the best, funniest and most scathing. But at the same time, it was done with the most love'.

Happy with his film experiences, Harrison was eager to make another one with Idle. And boy, did he!

1979: Father and Son

Although Harrison's marriage to Olivia Trinidad Arias wasn't perfect, it was nevertheless very happy. And just as Harrison took comfort in the many positive memories he had of John Lennon in the months after he was shot, Arias prided herself on what had proven to be one of the most successful unions in rock. She recalled: 'You go through challenges in your marriage, and here is what I found – the first time we had a big hiccup in the road, we came through things, and then you go, 'Wow!' There is a reward at the end of it. There is this incredible reward because you have lived through more and you have let go of something'.

Fatherhood had a positive effect on the erstwhile Beatle, especially coming so soon after the death of his own dad. Harold Harrison passed away in May 1978, having outlived his wife by most of a decade. George had three older siblings, and no one has suggested that there was anything but positive feelings among the clan. But burying a parent is a harrowing experience for any child, and at a time of great upheaval, Harrison's faith mattered more to him than it ever had. Like a flower emerging, growing over a protracted turbulent winter, Dhani Harrison entered the world: reigniting the spark behind his father's fading eyes. Dhani enjoyed a strong bond with his father, and knew him as a gardener; long hearing about any musical exploits his parent might've enjoyed: 'My earliest memory of my dad is probably of him somewhere in a garden covered in dirt, somewhere hot, a tropical garden, in jeans, khakis covered in dirt, just continuously planting trees. I think that's what I thought he did for the first seven years of my life. I was completely unaware that he had anything to do with music. I came home one day from school after being chased by kids singing 'Yellow Submarine', and I didn't understand why. It just seemed surreal: Why are they singing that song to me? I came home and I freaked out my dad: 'Why didn't you tell me you were in The Beatles?'. And he said, 'Oh, sorry. Probably should have told you that".

Dhani Harrison now acts as custodian of his father's legacy, and he writes his own material whenever he isn't espousing the virtues of the family heirlooms. Like Julian Lennon, Dhani agreed to represent his late father at a screening of Peter Jackson's newly-released *Get Back* documentary in 2021. Dhani was surprised by the results: '(My father) was always bummed out that this was portrayed in bad light, and they were always a bit sad about it, and that's why Peter has been given such a big crack at it. He's really delivered'.

In 1979, Monty Python – a group Harrison felt embodied the anarchic spirit of The Beatles – were working on their third feature, and had honed the script to make the biblical epic more contemporary in tone. Although superficially about a man mistaken as the Messiah, many of the script's more incendiary moments took a swipe at the political movements swarming all over Britain. Interestingly, one scene featured a male demanding that they be recognised as the woman they've always regarded themselves to be; the ending cutting into the flimsiness of friendship in the face of great upheaval. Between these set pieces comes a leper (or ex-leper, shall we say) who wishes to return to the life he had before being cured of his disease. Jesus Christ existed in this narrative, but the Pythons went to great lengths to not poke fun at a man they fundamentally recognised as an emblem of altruism. But the best joke is saved for last, as Brian resigns himself to crucifixion by joining his fellow convicts in a tidy, Broadway-style musical number. Brian's gratitude on discovering acceptance is delightful, although some audience members were upset by what they regarded as the Pythons mocking the very sacrifice that cemented their faith. In 1966, Harrison made it clear that religion was not beyond scrutiny ('If Christianity's as good as they say it is, it should stand up to a bit of discussion'), and though he had a similar philosophy in 1979, it's doubtful he would've financed a film he thought viewed religion in a negative light. If anything, *Life of Brian* had a cleaner message than the one John Lennon espoused in 1971 – the Pythons weren't asking people to imagine a world devoid of religion but to picture a world where viewers could chuckle at some of the more outlandish aspects of it.

But despite the sentiment, it was proving harder to fund, and after reading the script, EMI chairman Lord Belfont decided not to pursue it. Producer Michael Deeley (a proud practicing Catholic) disagreed with the concerns but could not persuade the mogul to change his mind, and *Life of Brian* returned to the folder of scripts from whence it sprang. Animator Terry Gilliam remembered: 'They pulled out on the Thursday. The crew was supposed to be leaving on the Saturday. Disastrous. It was because they read the script, finally'.

Spurned into action, Idle opted to call Harrison and inform him of their dilemma. He was intrigued by the project, not least because it was another Python vehicle, but that the resonances were so deeply cutting. Arguably the prototype for the seminal Irish series *Father Ted*, *Life of Brian* didn't set out to topple catholicism but to poke fun at people for following leaders blindly and uncritically. And Harrison – weary of fame since 1963 – felt this mindset matched his personal philosophy: 'I think that after The Beatles, Monty Python was my favourite thing. It bridged the years where there was nothing really doing, and they were the only ones who could see that everything was a big joke'. *Life of Brian* indirectly started Handmade Films, a company that would continue to produce features over the next ten years.

Michael Palin – regularly considered the most accomplished of the six Python actors – was pleased to hear that Paul McCartney would interrupt sessions at Abbey Road to catch the latest episode of *Monty Python's Flying Circus*. Palin said in 2019: 'I can't remember when I first met George. It's odd; it's like not remembering the first time you met the Pope or something like that. I think it must've been around the time we were setting up *Life of Brian*. I don't think I'd met him before that. We were just huge, huge fans of anything The Beatles did. George was a very good contact to have'.

So, Harrison agreed to finance the feature. What everyone wanted to know was Harrison's reason for doing it, especially when he'd devoted so much of his creative and intellectual energy into proving that a higher power actually existed. For him, this was an important factor, and he must've been amused by the central plot: about a simple man who stumbles (quite literally) into unwarranted fame. In many ways, *Life of Brian* continues the narrative *The Rutles: All You Need Is Cash* started, and though the soundtrack is sadly light on music, the film nonetheless ends on a cheery note as the congregation of people being crucified join together for one last sing-along.

In the face of death, music provided the answer. Blown away by the kindness, Idle took the time to praise the musician as he eulogised in the early 2000s: 'I think he would prefer to be inducted posthumously, because he loved comedians – poor sick, sad, deranged lovable puppies that we are. Because they – like him – had the ability to say the wrong thing at the right time: which is what we call humour'. Then he added that the 'funny' Beatle financed the most fondly remembered of the Python movies: 'Still the most anybody has ever paid for a cinema ticket'.

George Harrison wasn't the first rock musician to work on a film, but he may be one of the few who have openly resisted appearing before the camera. Okay, Harrison does pop up briefly in *Life of Brian*, but he wasn't financing a vehicle to showcase his music, as McCartney would on the ill-fated *Give My Regards To Broad Street*. Nor was *Life of Brian* an excuse to exercise Harrison's acting muscles, even though Richard Lester (who directed

A Hard Day's Night) thought he was a very good actor. Instead, he acted like the mentor Brian Epstein had been to him: nurturing hidden talent – particularly among artists who were struggling to get their voices heard.

On 17 August 1979, *Life of Brian* premiered in the United States. It ruffled some conservative feathers, but the critics adored it, with Roger Ebert stating, 'What's endearing about the Pythons, is their good cheer, their irreverence, their willingness to allow comic situations to develop through a gradual accumulation of small insanities'. It symbolised a watershed moment for comedy but also started Handmade Films on an 11-year journey that ended in 1990 with another Eric Idle venture: *Nuns On The Run*. Whether or not Handmade Films saved the British film industry is a debate this book doesn't have the word count for. But what's harder to argue against is the scope of the material, ranging from the alternative comedic rhythms of Withnail and I, to the schmaltzy romanticism of *Shanghai Surprise*. My personal favourite feature? All in good time!

At the start of the 1970s, Harrison was an ex-Beatle harbouring a voice that had been largely ignored for too long. By the end of the decade, he'd proven himself to be one of rock's most noteworthy polymaths; his influence gargantuan – and all from the confines of his 18th-century gothic mansion. All of Harrison's creative enterprises – from recordings of Vedic hymns to cinematic frolics captured in the Tunisian deserts – subscribed to the same school of thought, and each captured a person (traditionally a man) crying out to be the person they had always aspired to be. What each of these projects carried wasn't passion, but perturbation, as every character inhabited a failing that threatened to cut them down to their knees, and it was only through their undiminished loyalty to a higher power that they felt strong enough to carry on into the unknown future. In many ways, Harrison embodied every one of these projects in an effort to improve upon himself. And in a mere ten years, he'd shown he was something much greater than the grumpy guitarist who had stormed out of rehearsals during The Beatles proposed return to the stage. Instead, he fashioned a new image for himself, and one that was based entirely on the waves of time, considerate in his nature as both a musician and a person. Completing the triumvirate was his role as a father, and he was happy to impart knowledge to the child who now holds the key to his life's work. He favoured process over product and enjoyed watching seeds grow into something grander, no matter how long-lasting or influential the result was.

Depending on how you knew Harrison, he was many different things to different people, and while the interests of a film producer and a devotee have their superficial differences, they both stemmed from the same root that tied all Harrison's activities together: in the garden. 'I'm really quite simple', he wrote in *I Me Mine*. 'I don't want to be in the business full-time because I'm a gardener. I plant flowers and watch them grow. I don't go out to clubs. I don't party. I stay at home and watch the river flow'.

Harrison's extracurricular activity ended up becoming his primary port-of-call in the 1980s, and though he never stopped writing, his output steadily decreased as the years wore on. Incredibly, he only released four more studio albums as a solo artist (he did contribute to *The Traveling Wilburys*), and of this bunch, only *Brainwashed* measures up to the best of his 1970s work.

Cinema proved to be a more worthy use of his fans' time and attention, and Handmade produced several noteworthy pieces, the best of which is probably *The Long Good Friday*: a probing treatise on violence in a city drowning in commerce and creativity. Once again, it was Eric Idle who recommended the film to Harrison, and the guitarist went on to form a terrific friendship with its star Bob Hoskins. Hoskins is brilliant in *The Long Good Friday*: embodying a latent violence that's only hindered by his innate selfishness. In one tremendous moment of non-verbal acting, Hoskins demonstrates rage, fury and resistance, as a gun-toting Irishman (Pierce Brosnan, making his film debut) smirks knowingly at the kingpin. The silence works well on Hoskins, but he does sport a strong cockney accent, that was nearly overdubbed by an actor from Wolverhampton. Director John McKenzie recalled how difficult it was in securing a release for the picture, after Black Lion Films lost confidence in it on account of its violent nature. By the time the film was finally released in November 1980, it had lingered aimlessly in the mass vaults for some time, and would likely have been severely cut if not for Harrison's intervention. The film was rougher than the *Life of Brian*, but it too had a spiritual subtext – as another charlatan walks into the wilderness, aching to find some meaning and redemption in themselves, as the world abandons them to their own devices and misgivings. Seismic.

George Harrison

Personnel:
George Harrison: vocals, electric and acoustic guitar, bass, dobro, mandolin, sitar

Eric Clapton: electric guitar
Steve Winwood: Polymoog, harmonium, vocals
Neil Larsen: Fender Rhodes, piano, Minimoog
Willie Weeks: bass
Andy Newmark: drums
Ray Cooper: percussion
Emil Richards: marimba
Gayle Levant: harp
Gary Wright: Oberheim
Record label: Dark Horse
Recorded March-November 1978, at FPSHOT, Oxfordshire; AIR, London
Produced by George Harrison and Russ Titelman
Release datea: UK: 23 February 1979, US: 20 February 1979
Chart placings: UK: 39, US: 14
Running Time: 39:58

In 1979, Harrison released his sixth studio effort, and rather than tie it to
a mystical aphorism or a literary metaphor, he decided to name it after
himself. *George Harrison* was a sharper, more-sophisticated affair than
Thirty Three & 1/3, and showed that Harrison benefitted from periods
of creative interval. He sounded happier than he had in 1976, happily
recovered from the lawsuit that had discussed the similarities between
' My Sweet Lord' and 'He's So Fine'. At that time, he was still eager to
prove his worth as a songwriter, both within and without the Beatle orbit,
concurrent to practising meditation and slide guitar. And then marriage,
children and comedy entered his world, and he found himself engaging
with artists of a variety of ilks.

As his horizons opened, his demeanour was loosening, and he seemed
less proprietorial over his music. *George Harrison,* therefore, showcases
music for pleasure rather than music for art, and this lighter, more-
relaxed approach slipped nicely into the music. He sings freely, clearly
uninterested in pandering to anyone's thinly-veiled description of a
Harrison delivery.

By 1979 – with hit singles such as 'My Sweet Lord', 'Give Me Love
(Give Me Peace On Earth)' and 'Crackerbox Palace' – he'd mastered the
three-minute pop song, albeit one that skirted between detached irony
and euphoric joy. And on 'Blow Away', the famously moody musician
delivered what might just have been the merriest single any solo Beatle
had issued to date. Eager to jump on this newfound optimism, Harrison

agreed to appear in a promotional video for the single, and in stark contrast to the more flippant videos he directed with Eric Idle in 1976, 'Blow Away' showed the singer in various forms of delectation. There was the windup duck that stood behind him, the large swan that doubled as a toy and a boat, and then there was Harrison: jiving to the music like an unembarrassed parent at a family wedding. Rake-thin as ever, he nonetheless bore the appearance of a father, happy in the knowledge that his younger, more-carefree days were behind him. But age and responsibility didn't preclude him from having fun, and the 'Blow Away' video – sugary and stylish in equal doses – was the most fun video he'd yet produced.

'Soft-Hearted Hana' follows the example set by 'Here Comes The Moon', and returns listeners back to the world of The Beatles. But rather than wag another finger at the men, 'Soft-Hearted Hana' opened listeners up to a world where colours, chords and sensations were titillated by the composer's choice of drugs. Tempted by the fruit (or mushrooms) that took him to a higher plane, Harrison was reintroduced to the wonders of hallucinogens for the first time in about ten years. Recalling a journey to Hana in Hawaii, Harrison enjoyed the experience, although the drug's power was greater than perhaps he himself expected it to be. 'I nearly did myself in; I had too many', he recalled. 'I fell over and left my body, hit my head on a piece of concrete, but they were great'. The incident might've been painful, but it left him with a subject to tie an infectiously-hummable melody to. It certainly had its fans, one of them the album's producer: 'I went to Warners in Burbank and spoke to the three staff producers there: Ted Templeman, Lenny Waronker and Russ Titelman. And I played them some demos of the tunes I'd written and said, 'Come on, you guys, give me a clue. Tell me what songs you've liked in the past, what songs you didn't like. Give me a few ideas of what you think'. And they didn't know what to say. Templeman said he had liked 'Deep Blue' – the B-side of the 'Bangla Desh' single – which is a bit obscure, so I went home and wrote a song with a similar sort of chord structure to that: 'Soft-Hearted Hana'. But in the end, I decided I'd work with Russ Titelman'.

It didn't stop there – 'Soft Touch' was a masterwork of studio acumen, marrying Harrison's idyllic portrait of a Caribbean island ('...the wind, the cool breeze blowing, the palm trees, the new moon rising') to an eerie, evocative riff. The song seamlessly captured the blissful euphoria of a couple on holiday, as the guitars – swaying to the choppy rhythm – held shimmering, smouldering resonances. An exercise in controlled power and sparkling drum design, the song – like much of the album – felt like a continuation of his earlier work, and the riff did indeed stem from the horn section that cements 'Run Of The Mill'. More than that, the song was indicative of his standing in 1979, cheerfully reminding listeners that there was much to celebrate about the world: you just had to open your eyes.

'Love Comes To Everyone' is driven by a jaunty drum rhythm, pleasantly reminiscent of the fills Ringo Starr laid down for The Beatles in 1964. Harrison enters, caught in the fulfillment of the word-painting, and any vestige of dourness is swiftly discarded for a sprightly, shimmering guitar effect, leading listeners to the soaring chorus. But before anyone can accuse Harrison of pandering to the Beatles fans, he spent so long dissociating from; the slide guitar appears to remind listeners who it is they are listening to. The fusion of past and present is a common theme on the album, and with good reason too. With the burial of his father and the arrival of his son, the guitarist now stood amidst the changes that were the backbone of the religion that directed the adult in his search for individuality. And with 'Love Comes To Everyone', Harrison had produced his most beautiful work since 'Give Me Love (Give Me Peace on Earth)', continuing the narrative so central to his 1973 opus with greater expedition and resolve. The anger that had once drained dissenters on the uncompromising *Dark Horse* not only seemed like the writings of a younger man but a completely different one. 'I think what happened between this album and the last album is that everything has been happening nice for me', Harrison beamed. But amid all the synth hooks and polished guitar patterns comes a man as committed to his spiritual crusade as he always was. What changed wasn't the power of the message but the tone: now more pleased with the beauty both he and his generation had gifted to the world. In 'Love Comes To Everyone', Harrison recognised the challenges of life before surrendering his impulse to criticise others for their failings. Instead, he felt it his duty to applaud the world for it's endurance in the face of great adversity:

Got to go through that door
There's no easy way out at all
Still it only takes time
'Til love comes to everyone

If there was a god, it was a loving God, and Harrison was eager to celebrate this love at a time when he was enjoying tremendous good fortune. In an interview with *Penny Black*, Louise Harrison maintained that her brother's commitment to his spiritual pact was one that stemmed from childhood: 'It wasn't something that just suddenly happened when George got to a certain age. It was part of his entire life – to understand that the living part of us is the creator, and we've always believed that, so it wasn't like all of a sudden he suddenly became spiritual. It was part of his life from the beginning'.

Eric Clapton played on the track and even covered the song himself. But in a sea of musical cameos, Steve Winwood's appearance was the most noteworthy. Guesting on 'Love Comes To Everyone', the erstwhile Blind Faith frontman can be heard performing a scintillating synth solo during the instrumental section, the keys substituting for the protracted slide pieces frequently heard on Harrison's underwhelming 1976 effort. It was a welcome return to the soundscape of *Extra Texture (Read All About It)*, but this was a more jovial effort, and Winwood's keyboards only helped accentuate the laughter that was thriving within the track.

Of course, much of that was down to Eric Idle's influence. But Harrison seemed genuinely content in himself, probably more so than at any other point in the 1970s. His antenna was widening, and he was opening his audience to themes, topics and lyrics nominally considered atypical of the decade. ''Are you going to write a song about motor racing, George?' was a question I was asked a lot by various people from the Grand Prix teams', Harrison recalled, explaining the genesis of a particularly strange number. Buoyed by the challenge, Harrison gamely decided to translate his passion into music, and 'Faster' – a choppy number written for a younger generation of buyers – combined his passion for formula racing with the meditation that had stimulated his post-Beatles work. The rush that drove The Beatles onto Shea Stadium was making way for something more literal: motor racing – like singing, sex and spiritualism – was becoming an integral part of Harrison's person, and he was spending almost as much time on the roads as he was in the midst of prayer and answer. The result was a pounding ballad that could've become a radio mainstay had it been sung by a younger, trendier artist like Andy Gibb. But the result is ineffably charming, packing a whimsical, semi-western accompaniment. And unlike the turbocharged nihilism of the Manic Street Preachers' anthem of the same name, the song felt victorious, homely and deeply comfortable in the world it sat in. Harrison wrote in *I Me Mine*: 'Those drivers have to be so together in their concentration, and the handful of them who are the best, have had some sort of expansion of their consciousness'. What drama arises, doesn't come from the song, but from the sound of a slide guitar rescuing its master from a tricky corner. Harrison was older; more mature, but his guitar skills never wavered. As a composition, 'Faster' was a much more trendy effort than the more risible 'It's What You Value', and it might be his most successful ode to a vehicle. His guitar playing now contained an electricity that could only emanate from an artist caught in the impulse of his work. Harrison was in a very good plain creatively.

He continued to practice meditation, and those who visited Friar Park were astonished with the presence by which he maintained his personal life. The spiritualism – potent as ever – was pouring into his songcraft with great interest. His second wife Olivia recalled: '(George) always wrote of these things to remind himself. People sometimes accused him of preaching. But you know, he was really preaching to himself. He wasn't trying to say, 'You be like this because I'm already like this''.

Let's quickly turn back to 'Blow Away'. In his new form, Harrison was espousing the virtues of love: clearly unembarrassed by the subject. Listening to the track now, you can hear the giggles, laughter and good form that went into making it. Like much of his work, it grew from his desire to communicate with a higher power, although the conversation can also be read as a dialogue with his internal self, as it is a hymn to a greater force:

Sky cleared up, day turned to bright
Closing both eyes now the head filled with light
Hard to remember what a state I was in
Instant amnesia
Yang to the Yin

Unlike Paul McCartney and Ringo Starr, Harrison's work had rarely been written for the more mainstream buying audiences, and by that token, age had not weathered his influence on a particular fan base. What's most extraordinary about *George Harrison* is that it sounds effortlessly commercial, even though the artist himself was as apathetic to the charts as he had always been. As ever, prayer absolved him from the shackles of his past, leaving audiences to embrace the artist at his most fruitful, focused and forgiving. The album signalled another change for Harrison: It's safe to say that *George Harrison* wasn't a tightly-coiled, nakedly-confessional album in the mould of *Dark Horse*, but it wasn't his ticket back to rock stardom either. Fans eager for their hero to return to the world brandishing an electric guitar and an impish smile would have to wait for the release of *Cloud Nine*, and Harrison spent much of the 1980s secluded from the public, with nary a single or an album to gift to the fans. Small wonder he sounded so inspired on this album: it was his way of wrapping up one aspect of his life before clambering onto another.

George Harrison is the sound of a man who is stress-free, jolly and enjoying the simple pleasures of life. Not only was Harrison fully aware of his place in life, but he was also happier still to grab it. Ultimately, *George Harrison* demonstrated that hooks, choruses and tight guitar passages weren't beneath him, and like McCartney before him, he seemed comfortable enough to let his fatherly status guide the work, giving it a refined, even mature quality.

'Blow Away' was the obvious single, although the album also holds another formidable love song. From the buzz saw opening to the soaring chorus, 'Your Love Is Forever' was a richly-produced effort. Like Dylan, Harrison didn't hang his lyric on an individual metaphor, but rather let the narrative unfold in a series of endearing escapades. Bearing in mind the subject matter, the song had already proven itself in its barest, most rustic form. But laced with the central lick, the recording had a warm, even whimsical quality that made it sophisticated, singular and deeply respectful of its milieu. These were the best songs Harrison had written in some time, and completed a collection that proudly stands among the best of his catalogue. Arias adored 'Your Love Is Forever', and measured it among her husband's strongest works. She revealed in 2017: 'Those times in your life when everything is just smooth and beautiful, and you can really be your best self and who you want to be'.

Producer Russ Titelman enjoyed the process of the recording immensely: '(George) was a craftsman of the highest order, and he remains that kind of player in his solo music. The fluid approach he got from India was in songs on *George Harrison* like 'Dark Sweet Lady', 'Love Comes To Everyone' and 'Blow Away', which is a phenomenal pop single. A lot of people don't realize that 'Blow Away' used the rebuilding of Friar Park – the broken-down nunnery that he restored as his family home – as a metaphor for how he had to rebuild his life after The Beatles broke up and his marriage to Patti Boyd ended'. The producer did concede that Harrison needed a 'push' on occasion, but he was happy with the results. Titelman says in *Behind The Locked Door*: 'He lived in his own world, and I think he knew that too. He had the demos and he invited me over to his house in Benedict Canyon to listen. 'Blow Away' was on there and it sounded like a hit, and 'Love Comes To Everyone', which seemed like a pop record. 'Faster' and 'Not Guilty'. He had just the guitar part to 'Your Love Is Forever', no vocal, no lyric, but I was floored by it. I just thought it was the most beautiful thing, and I said, 'Look, you have to finish this song; we need this song for the record, so please write a lyric'. And he did'.

Superficially, the *George Harrison* album may sound sparse, but it's actually denser than you might think. And though the lyrics are meditative, the guitars are tight and punchy, and the effervescent sound landscapes do enough to disguise a backdrop that's rollicking and unrelenting. Between the instrumental passages, Harrison adopts a vocal style that's sincere and rapturous; clearly the happiest he's been singing on an album since 1973. On 'Here Comes The Moon', simplicity takes priority over style, lacing listeners in the importance of the moment:

Everybody's talking up a storm
Act like they don't notice it
But here it is and here it comes

It wasn't the first time he'd name-checked The Beatles on a song ('Living In The Material World' and 'This Guitar (Can't Keep From Crying)' are two other examples), but this wasn't mere fan-servicing – rather it was a sincere tribute to the power the night had on his creativity. And as he pointed out in an interview, no one else had written an alternative to 'Here Comes The Sun', so why shouldn't he? 'Here Comes The Moon' was the stronger of the two songs, considering that it was rich with contradictions: the trembling power of the lyrics contrasted neatly with the fiery sing-along chorus. This song was decidedly more impetuous, more longing and more tuneful than the better-known Beatle ditty, bringing greater clarity to the man's personal philosophies. In other words, he was now better able to articulate the sensations emanating through him than he had been during his Beatles tenure.

Sadly, the album isn't perfect, and the record stumbles early when the lacerating 'Not Guilty' opens an argument long thought to be finished. Dropped from *The White Album* in 1968 (reportedly for its content), the song had lain dormant amidst a sea of demos that lay in Harrison's possessions. With its supercilious nature and general air of disappointment in the organisation that brought The Beatles to its knees, the song was never destined to be a favourite, and his decision to reprise the song (particularly in an era of deténte for the four songwriters) was curious. Even worse, the song lacked the galloping bass of the 1968 original, and listeners were forced to make do with a plodding, pedestrian jazz lick in its place.

This one bum note aside, the *George Harrison* album was a strong return to form, demonstrating a work that was as cosmic as it was effortlessly commercial. What's certain is that it was his most diverse album in years. It's an enjoyably starry-eyed journey, embodying a romantic nature that was rife with romance, reflection, response and repartee. He was happily embracing the treasures in his life with the fervour he had previously salvaged for the darker aspects of his life in 1974.

Suffice it to say that George Harrison was a deeply personal affair, so his decision to eponymously title it wasn't just tidy marketing but a testament to where he was in life. Harrison didn't give too many interviews, but what few he did give, highlighted his change of tone. The critics were certainly happy. *Rolling Stone* wrote: 'After several highly uneven LPs that saw the audience for his mystic musings dwindle dramatically, Harrison has come up with his finest record since *All Things Must Pass*'. *The Washington Post* too considered it an improvement on the four prior 'dreadful' LPs, and in 1981, *NME* critic Bob Woffinden wrote, '*George Harrison* is his most successful album since *All Things Must Pass*, and would probably have sold in its millions had it arrived at the beginning rather than the end of the decade'. In the US, album sales were largely encouraging, but it was harder to push in Britain. Measured against the backdrop of the punk movement, interest in The Beatles was waning and would likely have continued to do so in the 1980s if not for the senseless actions of a self-centred gunner. Even Paul McCartney – who had enjoyed a great artistic resurgence in the 1970s – was struggling to rebrand Wings as a tighter rock unit, and the brilliant but hugely derivative *Back To The Egg* scarcely made a mark on listeners grooving to Public Image Ltd and Talking Heads. But Harrison seemed happy with his album, and for an artist largely unconcerned with chart positions, that was more than enough. Listeners would not get to experience this level of creative spontaneity again from Harrison until *Brainwashed* in 2002, and closing out one part of his artistic trajectory; he was readying himself for the challenges of film production. Cinema, like music, requires tremendous focus and optimism, and through Handmade Films, Harrison had established a new voice and identity that would carry him through a more uncertain decade, as his music was gradually becoming more of a sideshow than an exposé of his soul.

Having spent the majority of the 1970s in a state of perpetual reinvention, Harrison's sixth work slowed the trajectory down, turning the focus from the future, back onto the experiences that had led him to this point of enlightenment. No one could have foreseen the actions of a senseless gunner in 1980, but every one of The Beatles was now treading down a more contemplative path, which would continue into the 1980s with great fervour. Paul McCartney was including more and more Beatles tracks in the Wings setlists, and when he announced The Concert for Kampuchea in 1979, rumours began to circulate that Harrison and Starr were set to join him.

And then there was John Lennon, who was beginning to approach the idea of recording a new album – one that reflected his mindset as both a househusband and a contented parent. Maybe it was love that pointed Harrison toward a more reclusive career, but he had been pointing towards that direction as early as 1975. Harrison told David Jensen: 'At the moment, I don't have any sort of band. I don't really have the plan to do that, although there's a part of me which would like to do some concerts. I don't know, maybe I will do that later'.

Though they wouldn't reform The Beatles until the 1990s, Harrison and McCartney did appear onstage together, with the ever-ubiquitous Starr drumming behind them. Weddings frequently bring out the best in people, and the three Beatles were in fine form as they watched Eric Clapton tie the knot with Pattie Boyd. We're using 'fine' in the loosest sense of the word (Weddings are a godsend for people aching for wine), but they were happy to perform to the crowd gathered. In keeping with the occasion, the *reunion* was buoyant, bullish and influenced by alcohol, leading Wings guitarist Denny Laine to be grateful that no one recorded the event. Shea Stadium it wasn't, but at least it showed that the three men enjoyed being in the same room again. Lennon's absence from the event had nothing to do with any ill-feeling he may have harboured: he simply wasn't in the country. And it seemed like Harrison's feud with McCartney – arguably the most vicious and certainly the most public of any Beatle fallout – was beginning to thaw. Harrison told *Rolling Stone*: 'Yeah, well now we don't have any problems whatsoever as far as being people is concerned, and it's quite nice to see him. But I don't know about being in a band with him; how that would work out'.

When Harrison released his memoir , *I Me Mine*, in 1980, many perceived it to be a procedural text, as opposed to the autobiography fans were clearly craving. Of The Beatles, John Lennon featured the most prominently, but that did little to appease him, having spent the best part of a decade in America. Lennon's solo work had long failed to match Harrison's – either for invention or prolificity – which might explain Lennon's outburst upon publication of Harrison's memoir – stating that his imprint on the younger Beatle was unrecognised in its pages. The pair were not on speaking terms, which anyone who had picked up a copy of *Rolling Stone* in April 1979 would've realised. 'I haven't seen John for a couple of years', Harrison admitted, before querying if the songwriter still laid down tracks, even as a hobby. Sadly, Lennon and Yoko Ono's *Double Fantasy* sounded like little more than the work of a hobbyist – boasting none of the wit, sincerity or energy that existed in Lennon's work with The Beatles. But it did suggest that Lennon was eager to embrace challenges, having spent much of the 1970s in semiretirement. In a game of catch-up, Lennon was writing an album for Ringo Starr, which Paul McCartney had reportedly signed up for. Whether or not Harrison would've joined the three men is irrelevant. Lennon was murdered outside his Manhattan apartment in December 1980, before that avenue could be explored.

A Handmade's Tale

Harrison bookended the 1970s with two major milestones: the end of The Beatles – still the greatest band Britain has produced – and the beginning of a company that was instrumental in the continuation of British cinema. In both categories, Harrison's role appeared to be perfunctory, as his contributions – compositional, conceptual and financial – seemed to serve the artistry of others, as opposed to the many brilliant ideas that swam in his own mind. And yet, the guitarist spent the intervening years harnessing a voice that was his alone, earmarking a back catalogue that includes ballads as wistful as 'Run of The Mill', 'Try Some, Buy Some' and 'The Answer's At The End'. Plunging himself into spiritual philosophy, Harrison emerged from the precipice as much poet as a preacher and echoed a piety scarcely heard in the echelons of contemporary stadium rock. What he did perform on stage was frequently too painful for mainstream audiences to sit through, but anything he did play was wet with his virtuosity, value and choice.

Born a Pisces, Harrison harboured both the creative instincts and the prevalent moodiness that is commonly found in a person associated with that sign of the zodiac. And much like the fish that symbolises a Pisces, Harrison seemed most content swimming in a direction he chose for himself. Among the waves that Harrison journeyed on came a series of gorgeous elegies, an exhibition of ardent guitar patterns, and the solo album that listeners all over the world (including this writer) consider the most accomplished any Beatle has yet unveiled. But by picking up two features, Harrison had unwittingly found a new outlet that could both entertain his creative muse and give him new focus as he walked into a more thoughtful – and arguably more mature – part of his life. Much as he did as a gardener, guitarist and entertainer, Harrison recognised the dual importance of laughter and spirituality in giving texture to the work. And with no great desire to return to the stage, he had another outlet to release his material under.

Throughout the 1980s, Harrison contributed musical numbers to Handmade filmes *Time Bandits*, *Water* and *Shanghai Surprise,* and even granted Bruce Robinson permission to use The Beatles' blistering 'While My Guitar Gently Weeps' in the brilliant *Withnail and I*. By 1987, Handmade Films was long-established as one of the United Kingdom's most fruitful film studios, and Harrison – long out of the musical spotlight

– was enjoying a late-career renaissance with drum-heavy rockers 'Got My Mind Set On You' and 'When We Was Fab'.

Handmade Films enjoyed their greatest success with *Mona Lisa*: a probing East End gangster film that featured Bob Hoskins at his most magnetic. Hoskins – nominated for an Oscar in 1987 – enjoyed a friendship with the guitarist-cum-impresario, and in 1988, Handmade produced the Hoskins' directed *The Ragged Rawney*: a kitchen sink drama that featured future luminary Dexter Fletcher. In 2019, Fletcher unveiled *Rocketman*: a soaring drama that celebrated another one of Harrison's chums in crisp kaleidoscopic cuts. Entrusting Fletcher with documenting his hairier life choices, pianist Elton John had long changed in his ways by the time the film came into production. Fittingly, his desire for change had come from some sage advice he'd received from Harrison: 'Stop putting that marching powder up your nose', Elton said, keenly aware of the guitarist's own battle with the drug. More impressively, the words had an effect on John, and as of 2019, he was nearly 30-years sober: 'The nose is still there!'.

Sadly, Harrison wasn't alive to see the film, nor was he around to watch the Beatle musicals *Across The Universe* and *Yesterday* demonstrate the band's pull on an entirely new audience. But he must've been aware of his importance in bridging the worlds of music and cinema, and in the wake of Handmade's foundations, more and more films expressed an interest in combining the two languages into one medium. 1990s valedictorian pictures *The Commitments* and *Trainspotting* were pleasantly aware of how important music was for young men searching for answers, while Guy Ritchie's gangster opus *Snatch* channelled the energy of the turbocharged *The Long Good Friday*. And then there was *Living In The Material World* – Martin Scorsese's heartfelt documentary, released ten years after Harrison's untimely death, celebrating the musician's foresight and precocious musicianship.

All Those Years Ago

In the wake of John Lennon's murder, many of the stars that had lit the 1960s with sparkle, had chosen to either reclaim the legacy or shy away from it. Paul McCartney opted for the former, decorating his 1982 masterpiece *Tug of War* with Beatles throwbacks. As if reclaiming the Beatles mantle, McCartney and George Martin laced the album with numerous callbacks, and Ringo Starr dropped in to contribute percussion to 'Take It Away'. Amidst the rockers on the album, stood 'Wanderlust' – a sprawling piano ballad, complete with the most sincere vocal McCartney had recorded since 'Maybe I'm Amazed'. And then there was 'Here Today': a sombre acoustic ballad that decorated Lennon's achievements in a series of reverent vignettes. There, McCartney showed a man prone to tears, laughter, anger and love: an appropriate send-off from one creative partner to another.

Harrison, too had written a tribute for Lennon, and McCartney joined him on the chorus for 'All Those Years Ago' (Starr also contributed to the recording.) While only the most hardened of fans would consider this reunion a triumph, it did much in Harrison's favour, and 'All Those Years Ago' enjoyed a sojourn on the *Billboard* charts before it was eventually displaced by 'Bette Davis Eyes'. Moreover, it showed that Harrison and McCartney were enjoying each other's company, and the pair showed up at Ringo Starr's wedding on 27 April 1981. Starr had been struggling to maintain a film career, and his musical career was also floundering. But the British papers could chortle at his efforts in marrying Barbara Bach, the most fondly remembered Bond girl of the Roger Moore era.

For this writer, Starr's performance in *Give My Regards To Broad Street* (1984) is one of the film's few saving graces. Unlike Starr, McCartney never looked comfortable on screen, and he wasn't willing to sit on the sidelines as Harrison had done. Instead, he worked with laureates Michael Jackson and Elvis Costello, creating some of the decade's most sophisticated pop tracks. Better still, he accepted that his younger days were behind him, and bought into the nostalgia, his 1989 world tour boasting some of The Beatles numbers that had been absent for much too long. Starr, too acquiesced to the stage format, forming 'Ringo Starr and His All-Starr Band': a vehicle that allowed him to sing and drum with other artists of his age group. Rick Danko, Jack Bruce and Graham Gouldman all got to live out the ultimate fantasy for a bass player: locking into Starr's drum rhythm.

Harrison also returned to the stage, in 1991, at Eric Clapton's bidding. Clapton's marriage to Patti Boyd had now dissolved, and more tragically, he was now grieving for a lost child. In a move that mirrored his decision to put *The Concert for Bangladesh* together, Harrison answered the bidding of a friend in distress and agreed to perform in Japan. Age must've mellowed Harrison, as this time he played the solo to 'Something' as he had on the 1969 original. Indeed, every track (from 'I Want To Tell You' to 'Give Me Love (Give Me Peace On Earth)') was unveiled like he was playing them for the first time, and his vocals – more confident than they'd appeared in 1974 – sounded as if he was singing for his life. Anyone hoping for an album on the back of the tour was set to be disappointed, as Harrison spent most of the 1990s secluded from the public eye. He did rejoin McCartney and Starr for *The Beatles Anthology* series and sat near McCartney as the bassist bade farewell to his wife Linda at her memorial service in 1998.

In 2001, Harrison supervised the release of a remastered edition of *All Things Must Pass* – a compendium that included five bonus tracks (including the achingly romantic 'I Live For You') and a re-recording of 'My Sweet Lord': a performance that showcased a more sensitive reading of a lyric written by a man basking in his life's achievements. Although he expressed concern at the reverb that burst through the speakers, Harrison nonetheless seemed proud of the album that had set his solo career on its course. It remains his finest work, and one that equals The Beatles sprawling body of work, for texture, contradiction, character and invention. Sales were encouraging, leading writer Peter Doggett to pencil the event as 'a previously unheard-of achievement for a reissue'. In keeping with the album's spiritual message, the reissue was the last achievement Harrison enjoyed in his life. His battle with cancer was growing harder to conceal, and however much he cloaked himself, news was spreading to the outside world. He later complained about his physician's misconduct, and his estate claimed damages on his behalf. Although he was known for his glib sense of humour, it's hard to imagine Harrison enjoying the irony of a lawsuit being won in his name, after he'd spent much of the 1970s fighting cases instead of writing, singing or meditating.

More happily, the faith that had centred him for most of his adult life helped him as he ventured into another realm. He died on 29 November 2001, surrounded by Dhani, Olivia and Ravi Shankar, in the comfort of a property that belonged to McCartney. McCartney likened Harrison's passing to that of a younger sibling, but he felt sufficiently confident in their renewed friendship to play at *The Concert for George*: the commemorative performance modelled on the more lofty Concert for Bangladesh. There, buoyed by the occasion, McCartney delved into 'All Things Must Pass', duly aware of the work's significance. Man must grow older, age and die, but it's his accomplishments that stand out as the scythe comes down. Each of us is remembered more for the work we do for others than what we accomplish for ourselves. And in that moment, the most successful songwriter of his generation was humbled by the foresight of a musician who had sung with him on the streets of Liverpool.

But life never began with The Beatles, nor did it end with them, and it's much more important to focus on the tides of life rather than highlight the grandeur of one particular moment in history. But much as it did in 2002, 'All Things Must Pass' remains a quietly moving reflection of life in the shadow of great change, written by a man who experienced change whatever path he took.

The most notable development since beginning writing this book was the death of songwriter/producer Phil Spector. He died in January 2021, reportedly due to complications of COVID-19. It would be unwise of us to commemorate the producer uncritically, particularly in light of his criminal record. Found guilty of murder in 2009, Spector was sentenced to 19 years to life in the California state prison system: a sentence he was still serving when he passed away. Considering Harrison's disdain for violence, it is highly improbable that the guitarist would've spoken favourably of the producer had he lived on, despite their exceptional teamwork. Tellingly, Dhani Harrison did not ask for Spector's approval when he remixed *All Things Must Pass* (which eventually came out in a sumptuously-packaged box set) in 2020. While Spector's actions later in life are indefensible, he was nevertheless one of the most innovative producers of the 1960s and spearheaded a production style mimicked by such celebrated craftsmen as Alan Parsons and Jeff Lynne.

So, perhaps we should let his ex-wife Ronnie Spector summarise the man she knew within and without the studio: 'As I said many times while he was alive, he was a brilliant producer, but a lousy husband. Unfortunately, Phil was not able to live and function outside of the recording studio. Darkness set in, many lives were damaged'.

As is evident in this book, Harrison didn't need Spector to help him launch a musical career, nor did he need The Beatles to make him feel complete as a person. The trappings of fame that inspire so many to become rock stars amused him, but it didn't enrichen the tapestry he designed for himself. Instead, he remained committed to his spiritual journey, making sure that his last step signified the end of his earthly journey. 'That was very – that's really what he was practising for,' Arias confirmed. 'It's like the Dalai Lama said something that really made him smile. He said, 'And what do you do in the morning?' He said, 'I do my practice, I do my mantras, I do my spiritual practice.' 'And how do you know it will work?' 'I don't. I'll find out when I die.''

Also available from Sonicbond

On Track series

Alan Parsons Project – Steve Swift
978-1-78952-154-2
Tori Amos – Lisa Torem 978-1-78952-142-9
Asia – Peter Braidis 978-1-78952-099-6
Badfinger – Robert Day-Webb
978-1-878952-176-4
Barclay James Harvest – Keith and Monica
Domone 978-1-78952-067-5
The Beatles – Andrew Wild 978-1-78952-009-5
The Beatles Solo 1969-1980 – Andrew Wild
978-1-78952-030-9
Blue Oyster Cult – Jacob Holm-Lupo
978-1-78952-007-1
Blur – Matt Bishop 978-178952-164-1
Marc Bolan and T.Rex – Peter Gallagher
978-1-78952-124-5
Kate Bush – Bill Thomas 978-1-78952-097-2
Camel – Hamish Kuzminski 978-1-78952-040-8
Caravan – Andy Boot 978-1-78952-127-6
Cardiacs – Eric Benac 978-1-78952-131-3
Eric Clapton Solo – Andrew Wild
978-1-78952-141-2
The Clash – Nick Assirati 978-1-78952-077-4
Crosby, Stills and Nash – Andrew Wild
978-1-78952-039-2
The Damned – Morgan Brown
978-1-78952-136-8
Deep Purple and Rainbow 1968-79 –
Steve Pilkington 978-1-78952-002-6
Dire Straits – Andrew Wild 978-1-78952-044-6
The Doors – Tony Thompson
978-1-78952-137-5
Dream Theater – Jordan Blum
978-1-78952-050-7
Electric Light Orchestra – Barry Delve
978-1-78952-152-8
Elvis Costello and The Attractions –
Georg Purvis 978-1-78952-129-0
Emerson Lake and Palmer – Mike Goode
978-1-78952-000-2
Fairport Convention – Kevan Furbank
978-1-78952-051-4
Peter Gabriel – Graeme Scarfe
978-1-78952-138-2
Genesis – Stuart MacFarlane 978-1-78952-005-7
Gentle Giant – Gary Steel 978-1-78952-058-3
Gong – Kevan Furbank 978-1-78952-082-8
Hall and Oates – Ian Abrahams
978-1-78952-167-2
Hawkwind – Duncan Harris 978-1-78952-052-1

Peter Hammill – Richard Rees Jones
978-1-78952-163-4
Roy Harper – Opher Goodwin
978-1-78952-130-6
Jimi Hendrix – Emma Stott 978-1-78952-175-7
The Hollies – Andrew Darlington
978-1-78952-159-7
Iron Maiden – Steve Pilkington
978-1-78952-061-3
Jefferson Airplane – Richard Butterworth
978-1-78952-143-6
Jethro Tull – Jordan Blum 978-1-78952-016-3
Elton John in the 1970s – Peter Kearns
978-1-78952-034-7
The Incredible String Band – Tim Moon
978-1-78952-107-8
Iron Maiden – Steve Pilkington
978-1-78952-061-3
Judas Priest – John Tucker 978-1-78952-018-7
Kansas – Kevin Cummings 978-1-78952-057-6
The Kinks – Martin Hutchinson
978-1-78952-172-6
Korn – Matt Karpe 978-1-78952-153-5
Led Zeppelin – Steve Pilkington
978-1-78952-151-1
Level 42 – Matt Philips 978-1-78952-102-3
Little Feat – 978-1-78952-168-9
Aimee Mann – Jez Rowden 978-1-78952-036-1
Joni Mitchell – Peter Kearns 978-1-78952-081-1
The Moody Blues – Geoffrey Feakes
978-1-78952-042-2
Motorhead – Duncan Harris 978-1-78952-173-3
Mike Oldfield – Ryan Yard 978-1-78952-060-6
Opeth – Jordan Blum 978-1-78-952-166-5
Tom Petty – Richard James 978-1-78952-128-3
Porcupine Tree – Nick Holmes
978-1-78952-144-3
Queen – Andrew Wild 978-1-78952-003-3
Radiohead – William Allen 978-1-78952-149-8
Renaissance – David Detmer 978-1-78952-062-0
The Rolling Stones 1963-80 – Steve Pilkington
978-1-78952-017-0
The Smiths and Morrissey –
Tommy Gunnarsson 978-1-78952-140-5
Status Quo the Frantic Four Years –
Richard James 978-1-78952-160-3
Steely Dan – Jez Rowden 978-1-78952-043-9
Steve Hackett – Geoffrey Feakes
978-1-78952-098-9
Thin Lizzy – Graeme Stroud 978-1-78952-064-4
Toto – Jacob Holm-Lupo 978-1-78952-019-4

U2 – Eoghan Lyng 978-1-78952-078-1
UFO – Richard James 978-1-78952-073-6
The Who – Geoffrey Feakes 978-1-78952-076-7
Roy Wood and the Move – James R Turner
978-1-78952-008-8
Van Der Graaf Generator – Dan Coffey
978-1-78952-031-6
Yes – Stephen Lambe 978-1-78952-001-9
Frank Zappa 1966 to 1979 – Eric Benac
978-1-78952-033-0
Warren Zevon – Peter Gallagher
978-1-78952-170-2
10CC – Peter Kearns 978-1-78952-054-5

Decades Series
The Bee Gees in the 1960s –
Andrew Mon Hughes et al 978-1-78952-148-1
The Bee Gees in the 1970s –
Andrew Mon Hughes et al 978-1-78952-179-5
Black Sabbath in the 1970s – Chris Sutton
978-1-78952-171-9
Britpop – Peter Richard Adams and Matt Pooler
978-1-78952-169-6
Alice Cooper in the 1970s – Chris Sutton
978-1-78952-104-7
Curved Air in the 1970s – Laura Shenton
978-1-78952-069-9
Bob Dylan in the 1980s – Don Klees
978-1-78952-157-3
Fleetwood Mac in the 1970s – Andrew Wild
978-1-78952-105-4
Focus in the 1970s – Stephen Lambe
978-1-78952-079-8
Free and Bad Company in the 1970s –
John Van der Kiste 978-1-78952-178-8
Genesis in the 1970s – Bill Thomas
978178952-146-7
George Harrison in the 1970s – Eoghan Lyng
978-1-78952-174-0
Marillion in the 1980s – Nathaniel Webb
978-1-78952-065-1
Mott the Hoople and Ian Hunter in the 1970s –
John Van der Kiste 978-1-78-952-162-7
Pink Floyd In The 1970s – Georg Purvis
978-1-78952-072-9
Tangerine Dream in the 1970s –
Stephen Palmer 978-1-78952-161-0
The Sweet in the 1970s – Darren Johnson
978-1-78952-139-9
Uriah Heep in the 1970s – Steve Pilkington
978-1-78952-103-0
Yes in the 1980s – Stephen Lambe with David

Watkinson 978-1-78952-125-2
On Screen series
Carry On... – Stephen Lambe
978-1-78952-004-0
David Cronenberg – Patrick Chapman
978-1-78952-071-2
Doctor Who: The David Tennant Years –
Jamie Hailstone 978-1-78952-066-8
James Bond – Andrew Wild –
978-1-78952-010-1
Monty Python – Steve Pilkington
978-1-78952-047-7
Seinfeld Seasons 1 to 5 – Stephen Lambe
978-1-78952-012-5

Other Books
1967: A Year In Psychedelic Rock
978-1-78952-155-9
1970: A Year In Rock – John Van der Kiste
978-1-78952-147-4
1973: The Golden Year of Progressive Rock
978-1-78952-165-8
Babysitting A Band On The Rocks –
G.D. Praetorius 978-1-78952-106-1
Eric Clapton Sessions – Andrew Wild
978-1-78952-177-1
Derek Taylor: For Your Radioactive Children –
Andrew Darlington 978-1-78952-038-5
The Golden Road: The Recording History of
The Grateful Dead –
John Kilbride 978-1-78952-156-6
Iggy and The Stooges On Stage 1967-1974 –
Per Nilsen 978-1-78952-101-6
Jon Anderson and the Warriors – the road to
Yes – David Watkinson 978-1-78952-059-0
Nu Metal: A Definitive Guide – Matt Karpe
978-1-78952-063-7
Tommy Bolin: In and Out of Deep Purple –
Laura Shenton 978-1-78952-070-5
Maximum Darkness – Deke Leonard
978-1-78952-048-4
Maybe I Should've Stayed In Bed –
Deke Leonard 978-1-78952-053-8
Psychedelic Rock in 1967 – Kevan Furbank
978-1-78952-155-9
The Twang Dynasty – Deke Leonard
978-1-78952-049-1

and many more to come!

Would you like to write for Sonicbond Publishing?

At Sonicbond Publishing we are always on the look-out for authors, particularly for our two main series:

On Track. Mixing fact with in depth analysis, the On Track series examines the work of a particular musical artist or group. All genres are considered from easy listening and jazz to 60s soul to 90s pop, via rock and metal.

On Screen. This series looks at the world of film and television. Subjects considered include directors, actors and writers, as well as entire television and film series. As with the On Track series, we balance fact with analysis.

While professional writing experience would, of course, be an advantage the most important qualification is to have real enthusiasm and knowledge of your subject. First-time authors are welcomed, but the ability to write well in English is essential.

Sonicbond Publishing has distribution throughout Europe and North America, and all books are also published in E-book form. Authors will be paid a royalty based on sales of their book.

Further details are available from www.sonicbondpublishing.co.uk. To contact us, complete the contact form there or email info@sonicbondpublishing.co.uk